T0162139

Sheela-na-gig: Sacred Celtic Images of Feminine Divinity
by Jack Roberts

©2019 Jack Roberts
ISBN: 9781934170793

Process Media
1240 W. Sims Way, Suite 124
Port Townsend, WA 98368
www.processmediainc.com

Design by Sean Tejaratchi

SHEELA-NA-GIG

Sacred Celtic Images
of Feminine Divinity

by
JACK ROBERTS

PROCESS

TABLE OF CONTENTS

PREFACE

"This image is so archaic and fundamental as to be all but forgotten in modern life. This is the as-yet undifferentiated Mother-of-Life-and-Death. Her self-exhibition has nothing sexual or lascivious about it, rather it is a reminder of something which to us liberated moderns is much more obscene and frightening. This is where you came from, and this is where you are going to."

—Nuala Ni Dhomhnaill, *Sheelagh in Her Cabin*, 1994

This is a book about the sheela-na-gigs of Ireland. Figures with similar characteristics can be found in other parts of Western Europe and in parts of mainland Britain, and while these will be referenced throughout this work, those that are found within the island of Ireland are the principal focus.

Sheela-na-gigs and sheela-like images are found in several parts of the western Atlantic fringe of Europe. Odd figures that may be related have been identified in various places around the Mediterranean, but there are few that are anything like those found in Ireland and parts of Gaelic/Celtic Britain. By far, the greatest majority of the figures are found in Ireland, and it could be said that the only true sheela-na-gig is an Irish sheela-na-gig, for the name is Irish. As well, only a few figures found in Ireland were described by that name before it became the generic description for this type of image in the latter half of the nineteenth century.

On mainland Britain, most sources catalog about eighty figures. The majority of them are found on Romanesque churches from the eleventh to thirteenth centuries, and as such, they are more correctly classed as acrobatic or exhibitionist figures that largely lack the symbolic imagery and broad expressiveness of the Irish Gaelic/Celtic sheela-na-gigs. Fewer than a dozen are comparable, and these appear to be post-thirteenth-century, which makes them contemporary with the majority of the Irish figures. But most importantly, there is a contextual difference because nearly all of these lie within areas of Gaelic/Celtic or Nordic/Viking influence. By comparison, probably fewer than ten of the Irish figures appear to originate from the Romanesque period, before the thirteenth century.

Within Ireland, because of its particular adherence to tradition, an essence of what the sheela-na-gigs originally represented has managed to survive. Naturally, their story may still be somewhat fragmented and sometimes obscure, but within the myths, legends, and folklore, there is sufficient material for us to start to unravel their mystery and begin to see the remarkable, once highly revered sheela-na-gigs in their true light.

CHAPTER ONE

THE SHEELA-NA-GIG PHENOMENON

SHEELA-NA-GIGS are carvings of naked female figures posing in a manner that is usually described as "exhibiting" themselves and are often called obscene images, so it is rather surprising that they are found on churches and other religious structures. Even more surprising is the fact that they are not hidden or put somewhere they could be missed but are usually placed in the most prominent and visible positions, where everyone could see them, such as above the main doorway or over a prominent window. Sheela-na-gigs were sometimes erected on old town walls, near their entrances, but mostly they were carved onto quoins or cornerstones—some set sideways or laying down but almost always placed in so that they would be clearly seen.

Putting an image as bizarre and provocative as a sheela-na-gig above the doorway of a church, in the very place where an image such as the Virgin usually sits, seems totally incongruous, perhaps blasphemous, and so it is not surprising that there have been mixed reactions to them. It was originally presumed that they are pagan images, preserved for some reason by the church, but it soon became clear that they are in fact religious icons created specifically for a Christian church during the deeply religious era of the Middle Ages.

Until recent years, sheela-na-gigs have been regarded as interesting and somewhat enigmatic oddities, one of the many mysterious objects you find in

Sheela-na-gig on the Medieval Town Wall at Fethard, County Tipperary.

association with medieval buildings, a curiosity that might stimulate speculation but is not to be taken too seriously. To Michael Ryan, Keeper of Irish Antiquities at the National Museum of Ireland from 1979 to 1992, they were merely "a footnote to history." On closer examination, however, and after looking at all the factors related to them, it appears that those strange and enigmatic sheela-na-gigs are not merely fascinating curiosities, but extremely important archaeological artifacts that pose vital questions about the culture of the period within which they were created—and the true nature of Christian religion that existed during the Middle Ages.

As far as we can tell, almost all of them seem to have been created between the twelfth and seventeenth centuries, with the majority having been carved between the thirteenth and the sixteenth—the main era of expansion in the construction of monastic centers and large fortified castles or tower houses. As incongruous at it may appear, this is the very time when the Roman church appears to dominate almost all aspects of life in the region, and imposing its strict moral code and condemnation of sexual sin was high on the agenda. Sheela-na-gigs simply should not be there, and the fact that they are challenges everything we think we know about the history of Christianity, especially that of the Gaelic/Celtic lands on the western fringe of Europe.

These strange images raise a whole host of hugely important issues regarding the medieval Gaelic/Celtic church, challenging our understanding of the real beliefs of the people and clergy of that era—and most importantly our understanding of the role and standing of women in medieval societies.

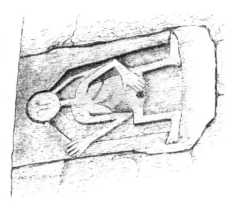

Sheela-na-gig on Clomantagh Castle, County Kilkenny. It is unknown why some figures were set lying on their side.

Sheela-na-gigs have usually been referred to as fertility images, protective talismans, or good luck symbols throughout history. But in recent years, the suggestion that they were put on the churches as "warnings against sin and lust" has found favor, despite the fact that the images themselves do not in any way suggest this as their function. Their original meaning and purpose is much deeper, and they are more significant than merely being gratuitous good luck symbols or some kind of inverted warning against sex.

Despite the "obscenity" of the figures, it seems that, according to tradition, the sheela-na-gigs had very little to do with sex and that such an interpretation of them as sexual objects is probably just a reflection of the repressed attitudes of the recent historical era.

To us in the present day, their meaning has been lost, but once we start to understand something about the true nature of the culture that created them, we can begin to see them in their original context. It is quite clear that they were deliberately placed on the medieval churches for a specific reason and with a very real purpose, and as such, they would have been clearly understood by everyone at the time they were placed there.

The story of the sheela-na-gigs is not so much one of deep dark mystery, though. Of course, there is so much we have yet to understand about them, but rather, their story is one of miraculous survival of something that, according to the conventional view of history, just should not be there. By being there, they demand that we reappraise our preconceived notions of the world that created them.

Left: The serene Sheela-na-gig from Ballylarkin Church, County Kilkenny.
Right: The Cavan Sheela-na-gig.

All historical reference to the sheela-na-gigs and traditions relating to them indicate that they were very revered images that held a high position within the religious iconography of the church. As a result, their existence serves to remind us of something deeply significant—especially in the present day, when the true nature of Christianity as followed by those of the old Gaelic/Celtic culture is finally starting to be revealed.

Sheela-na-gigs are called by various names, such as hags, cailleachs, or crones, and we tend to think of these words in disparaging terms, as they conjure up images such as an ugly old witch. But the word hag actually derives from "holy" or "hallowed (haloed) one," while crone stems from the word "crowned"—and the Cailleach is one of the most respected primary goddesses of Gaelic mythology. All of these names are essentially describing wise women, while the name witch is derived from Old English and is thought to mean "wise one."

CHAPTER TWO

IMAGES OF LUST AND THE ROMANESQUE QUESTION

IF YOU LOOK UP "sheela-na-gig" on the internet, there is an almost certain chance that the first image that will come up is that of the figure from the Church of St. Mary and St. David in Kilpeck, Herefordshire. This leering little figure, who is impudently pulling apart a large vaginal opening with both hands, is on virtually every website and every book about the sheela-na-gigs—as well as almost anything to do with the sacred feminine. She is used almost to the exclusion of all the rest of the figures, and yet she is not really a sheela-na-gig. She is more correctly classed as an exhibitionist or acrobatic figure—one of the many hundreds of strange human, animal, and bestial figures found on the highly ornate Romanesque churches, some of which are female.

The figure at Kilpeck is one of many similar early carvings found on the Romanesque churches of the tenth to the thirteenth centuries, the period before the appearance of the fully formed sheela-na-gigs in the later Middle Ages. What these figures are and whether they influenced the creation of the later sheela-na-gigs is central to the investigation of the phenomenon, as well as

The famous Kilpeck "sheela," Herefordshire, England.

being the most contentious issue in the whole debate over the meaning and purpose of the sheela-na-gigs.

It all started with Danish researcher Jorgen Andersen who, after seeing what appeared to be images similar to the sheela-na-gigs among the art on the early Romanesque churches of northern France, suggested that "the idea could well have originated on the continent." In his seminal 1977 work *The Witch on the Wall*, Andersen listed eleven such figures and suggested that these were the precursors to the sheela-na-gigs. His basic theory was that they were one of the motifs brought to Britain and Ireland by the Normans in the eleventh and twelfth centuries as a part of the influx of the Roman-style religious orders who introduced the idea into the Gaelic/Celtic world. Unfortunately, this also suggests that their meaning and purpose was possibly intended to promote church doctrine, which has resulted in the incorrect belief that they represent a negative, anti-sexual message.

There are certain merits to the idea that the Romanesque sheela-type image was in some way responsible for the original idea of creating the later sheela-na-gigs. The explosion of art on the very ornate Romanesque churches would have been of great influence in exposing the artists of the Gaelic/Celtic world to hitherto unknown forms of expression. These earlier sheela-like female images are, however, clearly quite different from the sheela-na-gigs that appear throughout the later Middle Ages. So, although it's very possible that the original idea was engendered by the Romanesque artists' imagination, the true sheela-na-gig is a more complex image. A real sheela-na-gig expresses far more than any of the earlier Romanesque figures, indicating that their purpose and meaning had totally changed.

Exhibitionist figure in column,
Normandy, France.

Andersen doubted that most of the Romanesque figures could really be classified as sheela-na-gigs because, in his view, they are acrobatic or exhibitionist figures—an "undecipherable class of Romanesque design" that are only displaying their vulvae as an "incidental aspect rather than as a deliberate gesture." The Romanesque sheela-like figures lack the complex symbology of the true Gaelic/Celtic sheela-na-gig, and there are few that are comparable to those carved between the fourteenth and seventeenth centuries.

The main question is whether or not there's a direct connection between the Gaelic/Celtic sheela-na-gigs and the Romanesque figures. The main problem, however, is that the idea of a Romanesque origin has led to an interpretation of the sheela-na-gigs that denigrates them and obscures almost all of the more important questions that surround these wonderfully diverse figures. The theory that they appeared as a result of the Romanesque artists' imagination also infers that they are merely another of the many images created by the church, as part of the theological propaganda being promulgated during that era.

A decade after Andersen's book was published, two British researchers, Anthony Weir and James Jerman, seized on Andersen's suggestion. The two then embarked on a quest for a continental origin for the sheela-na-gigs through an investigation of the Romanesque art of the churches of western France. The primary purpose of this research was to establish a factual basis for Andersen's suggestions. But as the title of their book *Images of Lust* suggests, its main purpose appears to have been to establish a theoretical origin for the figures, based on an assumption that they had a negative function and

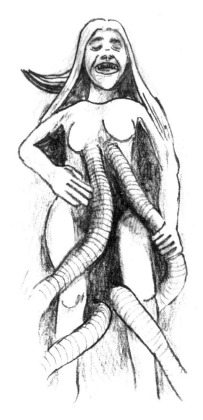

as such were placed on the churches as warnings against sin and lust.

Because Weir and Jerman were contracted to pursue their research and their subsequent book was published through an academic structure, their theory has, of course, found favor in such circles. As such, it's not surprising to see that it has been, and still is, the default theory to explain the figures, repeated again and again in journals and books since their book was released. Such a limited approach to the question of the sheela-na-gigs is woefully insufficient and does little to explain the use of the images that are found outside of the Romanesque context, and it has almost no relevance when examining the vast majority of the Irish figures.

Writhing serpents torment a female figure, Marnes, France.

There are literally hundreds of Romanesque churches in mainland Europe, and they are almost always quite remarkable structures. As its name implies, the architecture of the Romanesque era was a revival of the classical Roman architectural style, the main characteristics being the use of ornate semicircular arches for doorways, barrel vaults to support the roof, massive piers with aisles, and galleries.

Unlike the examples of later Gothic architecture, which began appearing in the thirteenth century, Romanesque churches have few windows but are highly ornate, lavishly carved, and brightly painted with a wide range of patterns. Most would have been dark inside, and except for small apertures, they were largely devoid of windows, deliberately creating a darkened otherworldly atmosphere that relied almost entirely on candles for illumination.

Romanesque churches are monuments to a revolutionary religious move-

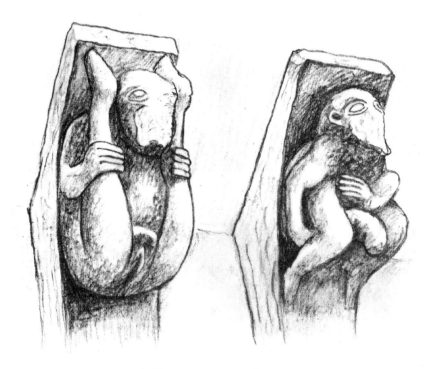

Corbel figures, Cervatos, Northern Spain.

ment that saw itself as heralding a new age of Christ, which expressed its zeal through elaborate church- and cathedral-building. They were masterpieces of artistic expression designed to impress and perhaps intimidate those who visited them.

In Ireland, the introduction of the Romanesque style was given one of its most influential endorsements with the completion of Cormac's Chapel on the Rock in Cashel—in 1134, three decades before the arrival of the Normans. During this period, both prior to and after the Norman incursions, many Romanesque churches appeared on the Irish landscape. Although most of these have suffered destruction down the years, many of the later churches rebuilt from their earlier constructions did retain some Romanesque features, such as the ornate doorways. Apart from the distinctly classical or Roman style of the architecture, these churches expressed a very unique fusion of Roman, Frankish, Germanic, Byzantine, and Islamic traditions. This is especially evident in the

The Nun's Chapel, Clonmacnoise, County Offaly, Ireland.

ornate patterns with which most of the stonework is bedecked, and the wide range of images carved into the capitals and corbels.

The array of images in some of the continental churches can be almost overpowering and incomprehensible. All kinds of faces leer and peer out at you, tongues protrude, people and animals strike odd postures or fornicate, writhing in pain or ecstasy. Among this array of symbolic representations are the so-called erotic figures, mostly male and usually with exaggerated penises, and some female figures, mostly naked and in odd positions: the exhibitionist or acrobatic figures that are misinterpreted as sheela-na-gigs.

There was obviously a greater trend toward evincing a fear of Hell and damnation among the populace of mainland Europe than there was among the

The Nun's Chapel, Clonmacnoise, County Offaly, Ireland.

Saxons, Gaels, and Celts. In the latter people's western lands, the images one finds are tamed down and certainly not of the same disturbing proportions as the continental Romanesque decoration. The Romanesque style in Ireland is even more distinctly Celtic in influence, largely consisting of arched doorways that are surrounded by heads and strange animal figures. But these designs feature very little that could be considered depictions of Hell and damnation— or even erotic images, such as are found on mainland Britain or the continent.

"Thou that enter gaze upon these divine things" is the inscription in Latin over the entrance to one continental Romanesque church, but the divine message that is most forcefully expressed appears to be that of damnation and Hell rather than divine salvation. The "lively compositions" of the Romanesque often appear to obtain their animation from the writhing and screaming of sinners who are suffering the torments of Hell. It's clear that the aim of these religious artists was to promote a sense of apprehension. High on their agenda was the depiction of acts of mortal sin. Neither murder nor torture, nor acts of rape and pillage of the kind that were concurrently being carried out under the order of Rome, but sex and sexual acts—in as many and various forms as it was possible for those medieval carvers to think up. Why they decided to depict acts of bestiality, sodomy, and extreme X-rated porn on the churches is open to debate. But it doesn't seem logical that they would have been effective as a warning against sex and lust.

Within that huge unbridled range of many thousands of carvings used by the Romanesque artists, Weir and Jerman list seventy female exhibition-ist figures in France and forty in Spain. None of these, aside from one or two exceptions, are really close contemporaries of the standing or squatting sheela-na-gigs of the Gaelic/Celtic world. Moreover, far from being inclined to show female exhibitionist figures, the continental artists deliberately de-picted phallic male images in abundance—so many, in fact, that Weir and Jar-man "gave up trying to count the male ones." Meanwhile, in Britain and Ireland, there are correspondingly few male figures.

The Romanesque carvings covering the churches of the continent, and to a lesser extent, Britain, may not depict scriptural motifs at all. At best, all we can deduce is that they have an unclear purpose. What is clear, however, is that the acrobatic female figure within this writhing confusion of Hell and weirdness contrasts sharply with the isolation of the later Gaelic/Celtic sheela-na-gigs.

Weir and Jerman list seven figures in Ireland that are associated with Ro-manesque buildings: Greyabbey, Aghalurcher, Toomregan, White Island, Rath-blathmaic, Liathmore, and Clonmacnoise. It is argued that these figures are of Romanesque origination and are among the earliest examples of sheela-na-gigs following the importation of the exhibitionist motif into Ireland. But the direct relationship between them and the non-Romanesque sheela-na-gigs is rather tenuous. For instance, the acrobatic figure whose face is embraced by her legs on the arched doorway of the Nun's Chapel at Clonmacnoise is set within a typical Romanesque ornament, but the carving is part of the overall decorative scheme within which it does not appear to have been given any ad-ditional importance. Unlike the bold positioning of the sheela-na-gigs, this lit-

Early Sheela-na-gig from Tracton Abbey, Cork, Ireland.

tle figure is almost hidden within the decoration of the arch.

At Rathblathmaic, a sheela-like figure is found alongside an ornamental carving on a late Romanesque window lintel that has been reemployed upside down. Although it is by no means a typical sheela-na-gig, it is a good example of the kind of early figure that could be a precursor to the later sheela-na-gigs. The same cannot be said for two figures from Greyabbey and Aghalurcher, as they are both thought to be male, while the figure from Toomregan is clearly slightly separate from the mainstream sheela-na-gig tradition, and its gender is rather ambiguous. A figure from White Island is another very curious inclusion, for although it was reemployed horizontally on a Romanesque church, it is widely regarded as pre-Romanesque—a possibly tenth- or eleventh-century carving that might be an early predecessor of the genre.

The main problem with any study of the Romanesque architecture is that there is such a wide range of images portrayed on those churches that one could ascribe an almost limitless variety of interpretations to them. From whence they arose and what they meant to the people who carved them and saw them is still largely speculation. Any interpretation of the female figures found in a Romanesque context that views them as anti-sexuality symbols derives almost entirely from church records, which show that Rome was promoting a kind of jihad against the old Celtic attitudes to sex. This was, however, mostly aimed at the clergy themselves, who were being forced to fall into line with the church doctrine of clerical celibacy, and it cannot be construed as an attack on the sexual morality of the common people.

If the female exhibitionist motif arrived in Ireland with the Romanesque architectural style, it is still not known whether this was as part of the same drive toward celibacy and church reform that was occurring on the continent. Possibly the motif was directly introduced by the European religious orders—such as the Cistercians, Cluniacs, Benedictines, and Augustinians—that were implanted in Ireland during the tenth through the twelfth centuries, which laid the foundation for the reform of the Irish church. This is supported by the fact that among the earlier wave of sheela-like figures are those found on Holy Cross and Tracton Abbey, which are Cistercian foundations, as well as Fethard (an Augustinian abbey) and Athlone (set up by the Cluniac order of the Benedictines in Ireland). This connection between the monastic orders and the sheela-na-gigs is not clear, and it's worthy of more consideration than we've been able to give in this work, as it may ultimately have a very important bearing on the whole subject.

Nonetheless, the late eleventh to thirteenth centuries herald a time of great changes and transition. The practices of the Irish Church, with its unique blend of paganism and Christianity, were coming under powerful pressure to conform to the European church. At the Synod of Cashel in 1101, Irish law was partially reformed by forbidding marriage between close kin, but it fell short of the requirements of Rome by failing to address the practices of concubinage and divorce. Such efforts toward reform were generally regarded as too little, too late, with Irish clerics stubbornly refusing to relinquish their traditional rights and celibacy, which remained an issue into the seventeenth century.

Irish civilization in the twelfth century, with its powerful roots in Celtic prehistory and a strong pagan tradition of mythology and folklore underlying its Christianity, was very different from that which had developed in most of Western Europe. It cannot be assumed that the motif from one country when imposed onto another retained any semblance of its original meaning. It is false to project the ideals and values of one culture onto another, and the fundamental question remains: If the clergy of Ireland were simply concerned about depicting lust, why did they not portray or copy the whole repertoire of carvings represented on the churches of northern France?

In Britain, the heavier influence of the Romanesque style has resulted in a number of sheela-like figures in more typical Romanesque settings. They are found primarily on corbels, chancel arches, capitals, and roof bosses. The more truly sheela-na-gig-like examples are the isolated figures placed in prominent or auspicious positions, such as the figures at Oaksey, Fiddington, Church

The sheela-na-gig in Church Stretton, Shropshire, England.

Stretton, Buckland, Croft-on-Tees, Easthorpe, Pennington, and perhaps most especially the figure at Llandrindod in Wales. These are among the most idiosyncratic examples in the whole repertoire and appear more closely related to the individualistic Gaelic/Celtic sheela-na-gigs than any of the Romanesque examples. Meanwhile, at Penmon on the island of Anglesey in Wales, and at Iona, the Scottish island outpost of an early Irish foundation, we find the insular type of sheela-na-gig, similar in style and context to the Irish figures.

The notion that the sheela-na-gigs were originally erected as warnings against the sin of lust to a supposedly illiterate populace is fraught with inconsistencies and does not make much sense, unless the carvings were fully visible. While the majority of the continental examples were carved on exterior corbels, in both England and Ireland, the Romanesque figures are often located in positions where it would have been almost impossible for them to be seen. An example of this is at South Tawton: A sheela-like figure is carved on a roof boss on the inside of the main chapel, where she would have been virtually invisible from below to the congregation. Likewise, the two figures from the twelfth- to thirteenth-century church at Tugford, in the west of England, are deliberately carved on the inside of the entrance door and, as such, could easily have been unnoticed by anyone passing them. It is also thought that the Romsey figure was erected on what would have originally been the inside of the church. According to a source of Andersen's, Professor Zarnecke, she is "in a place where it had no chance of being seen." In contrast, the Gaelic/Celtic sheela-na-gigs are mostly erected in very obvious places, such as over doorways, and even in the few instances where they're high up on a building, they're still clearly visible.

Corbel figures at Tugford, Shropshire, England.

Romanesque figures are almost always found as a part of a larger scheme of carved figures, while the Gaelic/Celtic sheela-na-gigs are isolated singular figures with no associated carvings. Within the larger schemes of Romanesque artwork, the sheela-like images do not have any particular significance, and there's an absence of tradition relating to them. Meanwhile, the Gaelic/Celtic sheela-na-gigs were highly regarded, very significant images to which a great deal of tradition was attached. Romanesque figures are only found on the churches of that period, whereas the Gaelic/Celtic sheela-na-gigs are found on churches of all types throughout the Middle Ages as well as on castles, town walls, et cetera.

What is clear is that once the sheela-like images arrived into the area of Gaelic/Celtic influence, and particularly when they arrived on Irish soil, it wasn't long before the distinct environment, with its unique mix of Gaelic/ Celtic and Anglo/Norman, led to them being enveloped in a native tradition, which did not necessarily view them as having a negative function. A separate classification for the Gaelic/Celtic and Irish figures is necessary, for although the Romanesque style may have influenced them, they are very much an indigenous product.

UNRAVELING A MISINTERPRETATION

In her book *Sheela-Na-Gigs: Unravelling an Enigma*, Barbara Freitag points out that to lump the sheela-na-gig-type images in with the vast array of grotesque Romanesque church imagery is to blur their distinction, rather than bringing them into focus. More importantly, it portrays the sheela-na-gigs as something to be feared, while in the Gaelic/Celtic world, they were most definitely revered.

Freitag states that "the categorical mindset [of Weir and Jerman] does not make a lot of sense. Apart from the implausibility of their line of arguments, it has to be said that their empirically derived interpretation—confined within the limits of art history and devoid of any spiritual dimension or recourse to other disciplines—fails to open new avenues for further exploration."

This is, of course, exactly what they set out to achieve: a final and irrefutable solution, a doctrine that would contain sufficient evidential examples, and a plausible enough theory to satisfy the need for an "academic solution." Unfortu-

Sheela-na-gig from Behy Castle, County Sligo, Ireland.

nately, being given such approval, the "images of lust" theory has become a misogynistic dogma from which the sheela-na-gigs have yet to fully emerge. There is, however, so much more to the story.

Although the limbs of many Romanesque female exhibitionist figures may be contorted or exaggerated to a greater or lesser degree, somewhat like a comic strip method of portrayal, the figures are still clearly pictorial representations of women. This is due to the fact that Romanesque art represents a fusion between the well-proportioned, naturalistic, clear-cut forms imported from Mediterranean art and the asymmetrical, convoluted, and zoomorphic compositions of the northern traditions. In contrast to the continental examples, the majority of insular sheela-na-gigs are often highly exaggerated and asymmetrical, as in the northern Gaelic/Celtic tradition. In fact, they're often barely recognizable as female were it not for their sexual organs.

The absolutely benign, otherworldly expression of the sheela-na-gig from the thirteenth/fourteenth-century parish church at Ballylarkin with sagging breasts, along with the peaceful-looking figure that formerly adorned Rochestown Church, hardly look like the artist is trying to portray woman as an image of evil, let alone one that conveys the possibility of damnation through sex. Their symbolism will be examined in much more detail later. But for the

Phallic exhibitionist figure,
Normandy, France.

moment, it's sufficient to note that if they cannot be recognized as representing real or even approximately lifelike women, then there seems little further basis that they seek to convey an anti-woman or anti-lust image.

It is evident that the carvers of the numerous figures that cover the highly decorative edifices of the Romanesque churches on the continent were skilled stonemasons whose level of expertise was of a very high standard. However, in Ireland and the Gaelic/Celtic fringe, although there were many skilled stonemasons around, the standard of carving the sheela-na-gigs varies dramatically, with some being very skillfully carved and others more crude or simplistic. As well as the workmanship being quite unequal, the style of the figures differs very much, and it's clear that the Gaelic/Celtic sheela-na-gig is not a mere copy of the Romanesque examples.

It seems probable that, in contrast to the figures carved by the continental stonemasons, the more unique and individual Gaelic/Celtic sheela-na-gigs were executed by nonprofessionals. These may have been local people, who were chosen perhaps for their magical skills over their sculpting skills, and who evidently had an arcane purpose in mind, rather than the desire simply to depict a sexual image. The theory that the sheela-na-gig originates as a Romanesque anti-lust figure actually brings to light even more questions and contradictions, which so far remain unanswered. For instance, considering the enormous range of Romanesque motifs, why did the Irish only import the female exhibitionist figure and not the male figures? Let alone all the other erotic figures, which the original carvers of the Romanesque clearly preferred? Why are Gaelic/Celtic sheela-na-gigs often the only form of decoration on a church, typically placed in prominent positions? Why do they never form part of a larger decorative scheme, as we find in the continental examples? Also, there is the question of why the majority of Romanesque figures are carved in an acrobatic posture, while the majority of the Gaelic/Celtic figures are standing or squatting.

It is possible that the later Gaelic/Celtic sheela-na-gigs have actually no connection whatsoever with the female imagery found on the tenth-century churches of Europe. But if they do, it appears that from a birth amidst the negative imagery of the Romanesque world, the context completely changed as the image spread into the Gaelic/Celtic world. It's been suggested that the Irish merely adapted their traditional images, influenced by both folklore and mythology, to the newly introduced exhibitionist motif. Having been encouraged into self-

Female exhibitionist figure, Normandy, France.

expression by the new symbolic art of the Romanesque artists, they "forged ahead with renewed enthusiasm, producing more and better sheela-na-gigs than anyone else."

The people of Ireland have always embraced innovative ideas. This is a deeply important part of the ancient and modern psyche and culture of the country. Ireland welcomed the earliest form of Christianity as early as the second or third century, and it was not imposed but willingly imported by the druids or brehons. All the new ideas represented by Christianity, such as writing and new forms of art, were eagerly accepted by the people of Ireland. Sheela-na-gigs are just another aspect of this ancient process. This neatly ties in chronologically with the transference of the idea of an image via the influx of new religious orders—which was, after all, the main purpose of the Norman invasions into Britain and Ireland. It may have some bearing on the subject but leaves open many pertinent questions. The first two of these are: Where on earth did they come from to begin with, and why would the idea spread throughout a clergy that was hellbent on removing women from the church, with the exception of the sanitized, virginal version of Mary?

The defaced figure, Périgord, France.

It is quite clear that the art and architecture of the Romanesque significantly influenced the way spiritual and religious ideas would be expressed over the centuries that followed. The highly ornate churches of the period would have acted as a stimulus that engendered a freedom of expression that was absent from the old Gaelic/Celtic world, which expressed ideas in more of a symbolic rather than representational form.

The sheela-na-gigs can then be seen as a mixture of the older, more symbolic forms and a new, more liberated sense of expression. Many of the figures have the same pear-shaped head with pointed chin that is used on earlier figures, while the rest of the image is depicted with a previously unknown sense of realism. If the sheela-na-gig image did first come into consciousness within the world of Romanesque art, there is still the question of where the image originated prior to the tenth century. Did those early Roman church artists simply invent the idea as a warning to the faithful against sin and lust? Or was it part of a mythical repertoire that already existed in the art and lore of the era from which the Romanesque arose?

Obviously, because they were on all those Romanesque buildings, those acrobatic exhibitionist figures were regarded by the church as innocuous. After all, they commissioned them, and there's no evidence of them being damaged or destroyed in the same way the later sheela-na-gigs were. Among all of the acrobatic exhibitionist figures found on the churches of France from the Romanesque period, one figure from the Dordogne region, which is now in the museum in Périgord and was illustrated by Andersen, seems to have some parallels with the later Irish figures. The original position of the figure is unknown, and it's unsure from which church it originates. But most striking is the fact that its face has been deliberately destroyed, while the rest of the figure remains undamaged. It seems strange that this one image, which is more closely compared to the Irish figures, should have had her face intentionally removed. Perhaps this suggests that, like the Gaelic/Celtic sheela-na-gigs, she represented something much more powerful—something that the church had no control over.

Whether or not the Gaelic/Celtic sheela-na-gigs have their roots in an image conjured up by Romanesque masons—and whether whatever was on the minds of those artists had any relevance to their meaning on the churches of Ireland—will probably remain a matter of contention. What's quite clear is that the sheela-na-gig that developed in the Gaelic/Celtic world signified something very special and far more significant than an obscure, ambiguous pornographic image. In the Gaelic/Celtic/Norman world, the exhibiting figure takes on its most extraordinary and challenging shape.

CHAPTER THREE

THE OLD GAELIC/
CELTIC CHURCH
AND THE SAINTLY
SHEELA-NA-GIG

IN THE GAELIC/CELTIC WORLD, the sheela-na-gigs are invariably the only decoration of any significance on the church or building they adorn, and they are almost always set in a clearly visible and prominent position, such as above the doorway. This indicates that they were not mysterious or arcane objects but something that was universally recognizable and understood. In her book *Sheela-Na-Gigs: Unravelling an Enigma*, Barbara Freitag places the figures in a commonly comprehensible position among local communities and states unequivocally that "here are plenty of indications that Sheela-na-gigs belong with ordinary people and rural traditions." If the local rural people recognized what they were, then there would surely have been little mystery or ambiguity about their meaning.

The main problem is that the traditions related to the sheela-na-gigs were kept very much among the common folk, and by the time records were made of them in the mid-1800s, they had been more or less lost or driven underground. When the first researchers came across sheela-na-gigs, they enquired about those rural traditions from the locals, but they do not appear to have gained much that would explain them. Andersen suggested that these Victorian researchers were "gripped with near apoplexy at the sight of them," and voiced his disappointment that the earlier researchers did not direct more research toward the subject.

For the latter part of the nineteenth century, speculation about the sheela-na-gigs predominated over investigation, and it was not until Edith Guest and her colleagues started to spend time with the rural

Killinaboy, a saintly image over the door.

people that a picture started to emerge about how they regarded them. From Guest's inquiries, it became clear that, without exception, the sheela-na-gigs were always considered powerful images and were very highly revered. Most significantly where folk practices have been allowed to continue relatively uninterrupted, there are several instances of them being regarded as images of special mythical or divine women. Perhaps most significantly, some were, and sometimes still are, thought of as actual images of saints.

It has been argued that this belief in the sheela-na-gigs being the image of a saint is merely a recently applied interpretation to explain away their existence and, as such, is of little direct relevance. There is a good deal of evidence, however, that a saintly figure as envisioned by people of former times appears to have differed quite dramatically from how this is usually imagined in the modern day. The figure at Dowth was known in earlier times as an image of Saint Seanchan, which is a curious and apparently dual-gender name meaning "wise one." In the west gable of the old church of Seir Kieran, another sheela-na-gig was regarded as an image of its founding saint, Kieran, which may bring into question the true gender of this presumed male saint.

Killinaboy, a saintly image over the door.

The Coptic Cross / Cross of Lorraine.

Two of the most important examples of sheela-na-gigs that were regarded as saintly figures are the one at Ballyvourney in County Cork and the one at Killinaboy in County Clare. Traditions were, until very recent times, very similar at both sites, and there is evidence to suggest a direct connection between them. At Ballyvourney, many pilgrims still visit the site and regard the sheela-na-gig as an image of the saint. At Killinaboy, although the traditional pilgrimage has not survived as strongly as at Ballyvourney, when Edith Guest visited Killinaboy, the local people she encountered at that time also regarded the sheela-na-gig as an image of the founding saint of the site, Inghean Bhaoithe (pronounced locally as "Innan Wee").

The sheela-na-gig at Killinaboy is situated right above the church's doorway, a position that renders her unavoidable to all who enter it. Unfortunately, she is becoming rather worn with age; photographs taken in the 1960s illustrate some features much more clearly than can now be seen, and there is a need for thought to its preservation.

Inghean Bhaoithe was the daughter of a druid, specifically the daughter of Boath, which may be an allusion to the great mother goddess Boande of the Boyne Valley, who is also known as the Cow Goddess. She is also closely related to a magic cow, the Glas Ghoibneach, which also features in the traditions related to other important saints, such as Saint Ciaran, also known as Seir Kieran. Inghean Bhaoithe is

The Romanesque cat figure.

also known as Saint Findelu, and she is not recognized by the church. Her status as a religious figure survives entirely because of continued veneration for her, which was formidable in the early Christian era, when she was known as the patron saint of the ruling Dál gCais clan of western Munster.

The site was formerly a major monastic center, but apart from the stump of the round tower and the local history relating to the site, little remains to testify to its former importance. However, some unique features survive at the site, which testify to the original Coptic roots of the old Celtic church. The present church was originally built in the eleventh century but considerably reconstructed in the eighteenth century, and one of its immediately noticeable features is the Cross of Lorraine, which is basically a Coptic cross, marked out in the stonework of the western-facing wall of the church. This feature indicates that Killinaboy is a very ancient foundation and represents an important remnant of the old Gaelic/Celtic church.

Inserted in the wall just inside the doorway is a remnant from the earlier period church: a classic Romanesque-style carving that has been retained in this way during the eighteenth-century reconstruction. It appears catlike, and there is a small cross possibly marking the genital

The Tau Cross.

The Ballyportry Sheela-na-gig.

area. There is another Romanesque carving, presumably also from the earlier church, inserted in the eastern wall of the graveyard. One other artifact connected to Inghean Bhaoithe, and another example of the ancient Coptic connection, is the unique Tau Cross with two faces carved on its upper surface. It was originally erected about 1.5 kilometers to the northwest, close to the road to Kilfenora, and is now marked by a replica, the original being housed in the Heritage Centre in Corofin.

The earliest forms of Christianity did not arrive into the Gaelic/Celtic lands as the result of missionary zeal. It had been well known in Ireland long before the arrival of the legendary Saint Patrick, and the earliest saints were actually the sons and daughters of old chiefs and kings, from high-class bardic families. These were quite obviously people sent specifically to special places of learning in order to bring it back to Ireland. It is clear that the early form of Christianity, with its mixed monastic communities and the popularity of remote hermitages in places such as Skellig Michael, was a Coptic style of Christianity with Gnostic roots. Evidence of this is widespread, especially in the western parts of Ireland, where traditions as well as actual artifacts are a testament to the ancient Coptic lineage that lies at the heart of the Gaelic/Celtic Christian tradition.

In the area within a few miles of Killinaboy, there were originally three sheela-na-gigs: one aforementioned, one formerly adorning the small castle of Ballyportry about 1.5 miles or two kilometers east of Corofin (now in the Clare County Museum in Ennis), and a third figure that is still in situ on the old monastic site of Rathblathmaic about two miles or three kilometers to the south of Corofin. These three sheela-na-gigs are fairly closely connected and the only known sheela-na-gigs in this part of the county, which suggests that it was an center of traditional Gaelic culture during the medieval era.

The carved window lintel, Rathblathmaic.

The sheela-na-gig in the ruins of the old church at Rathblathmaic is one of the smallest in the country and forms part of a Romanesque-style decorated window lintel that has been reused from an earlier church. Curiously, the lintel has been inserted in the wall upside down. The style of the figure is somewhat similar to the sheela-na-gig in the round tower at Ratoo (Kerry 92) but with more pronounced features and a raised right arm. The carvings on the Rathblathmaic stone have been related to a serpentine ornament found on a late Romanesque window at Annaghdown, County Galway, dated to 1180, and a Scandinavian origin has also been suggested.

The monastic center of Rathblathmaic was originally quite extensive, and there remains of a round tower have been identified, which suggest a much larger foundation. Although we have no record of the saintly figure after whom the church is named, it seems that he or she is another "folk saint" like Innan Bhoaithe. The name suggests that it is built on an ancient rath or ring fort named after her or him, which strongly suggests a pre-Christian origin. It is a prominent location on a high ridge overlooking Rath Lake, which in tradition was inhabited by twenty-five banshees who washed the clothes of those doomed to die. The lake was formerly known as Lough Briocsighe (Badger's Lake), after a fearful badger-like monster that dwelt there until it was subdued by Sain Mac Creiche, from Liscannor, who was famed for slaying troublesome monsters and demons.

A RUB OF THE RELIC

In the traditional world, there appears to be little distinction between the pagan deities and the Christian saints, and although the picture painted by the church of the pious saintly figure may be keen to distinguish itself from the pagan elements, it appears evident that to the people of former times, those saintly figures would have been liberally colored with the elements of their pagan predecessors. A sheela-na-gig erected on a church, which may at first seem totally inconsistent with its teachings, appears a more appropriate symbol and less inconsistent with people's beliefs than might be supposed.

Whether it was the original intention of the carvers to depict an image of the local founding goddess-turned-saint or a later belief that became attached is not known. But it is certainly most intriguing that a number of Irish sheela-na-gigs became associated with the same magical, healing fertility and talismanic powers attributed to the female saints—and the main way in which this healing power is transferred is by rubbing the sacred object.

Objects considered holy, whether they are remains like the bones of saints, or articles believed to relate to them in some way, are considered to have certain fertility or healing powers. Rubbing or touching such objects of veneration is a tradition that is probably as old as religion itself. Indeed, it is such a common practice to rub any items associated with saintly figures that a "rub of the relic" is one of the more common Irish sayings. Evidence of rubbing can be seen on a widely distributed range of sheela-na-gigs in both Ireland and Britain, the rubbing being almost entirely concentrated on the vulva. Many of the sheela-na-gigs have vulvae so well polished

The Buckland figure, now out of reach.

that it is evident they have been
rubbed over a considerable period. This is so common that it is
likely that all of the figures that
were within reach would have
been touched or rubbed in this
manner.

At Buckland in England, the
sheela-na-gig has received con-
stant rubbing of her vulva, leaving a deep hollow, and interestingly, it looks as if the fingers
have been re-incised. At Clenagh
Castle, the sheela-na-gig carved
on a quoin stone set close to the
ground is a later, spindly figure,
on which the pudenda are indicated by an oblong, diamond-
shaped depression. This also shows some signs of rubbing, perhaps performed
before entering the building.

Ballyvourney, the Sheela-na-gig
above the window.

The veneration of saintly objects by rubbing them can be seen at almost
all of the old holy places in Ireland, but at the ancient, venerated site of Ballyvourney in County Cork, the practice includes a whole range of saintly objects,
including a sheela-na-gig. Ballyvourney is widely renowned as the site of a
monastic center established by Saint Gobnait, and even today, a great number
of people still travel long distances to visit the holy site. The sheela-na-gig has
been carved in relief in an oval recess, which is set at an unusually odd slant
in a reemployed window lintel. The top half of the figure is in a relatively good
state of preservation, with the hands clearly pointing toward her lower abdomen or genital area. However, the lower half is very obscure, and although the
legs are missing, it appears as if the figure is standing. To the pilgrims, this
small, benign-looking sheela-na-gig is traditionally considered as an actual
image of Saint Gobnait.

At Ballyvourney, the sheela-na-gig constitutes an integral part of the ritual at the site. Votaries encircle the old church, walking sun-wise and pausing

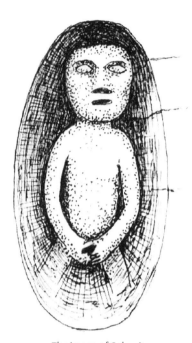

The image of Gobnait.

The sacred ball in the wall.

at several places of special virtue, which includes a niche in a wall in which a smooth round agate ball has been inserted as well as the sheela-na-gig above the window, each of which is rubbed. On the saint's feast day, other items are put on display in the nearby church—relics that are considered special items belonging to or related to the saint. These include an ancient wooden statue, which used to be carried around dressed up in rags, in exactly the same manner as the corn dollies that were made on Saint Brigit's Day.

The legend attached to Gobnait's ball is that the saint objected to a local chief building a castle near her abbey, so she threw her ball at the walls each night, whereupon what had been built during the day fell down. A few sheela-na-gigs are depicting holding round balls or discoid objects, which perhaps represent such balls of Celtic saints used for a variety of tasks, such as cures or for swearing oaths.

The most highly revered artifact at Ballyvourney is an ancient wooden image said to be of the saint. The antiquarian John Windele wrote about it being attacked by the local priest on account of it "leading to undesirable practices," but the people concealed it. In the 1840s, a representative of the traditional keepers of the shrine, the O'Herilihys, also known as "Gobnait's Clergy," handed it over to the parish priest, and it is now located in inside the parish church, and only brought out on Gobnait's feast day.

A traditional ritual attached to the wooden statue is that it is measured with ribbons and, like the sheela-na-gig, the figure is then rubbed, but here, it is done lengthwise along the body. This measuring and rubbing transfers the power of the statue to the ribbon, which then becomes a *tomhas Gobnatan* or Gobnait's Measure, and is thereby able to effect cures. Pilgrims also rubbed their afflicted limbs on the statue, and in contrast to the supposed fertilizing power of the sheela-na-gig, a handkerchief rubbed around the neck of the wooden image could also be used as a prophylactic.

At Ballyvourney, we can still see devotees following ancient customs that have all the hallmarks of having changed little over countless generations. The sheela-na-gig is clearly regarded as an image of Saint Gobnait and has for a long time existed as an important constituent element—and in the absence of any other explanations, there seems no reason to suppose that it should ever have been regarded as anything else.

Gobnait in particular shares many of the same attributes as Saint Brigit, in particular the restoration of health, fertility, and protection against illness. Seamus O'Catháin, who has written extensively on the subject of Brigit, not only connects Gobnait with Brigit, but regards them as being 'one and the same person' and notes that Gobnait's feast day falls on 11th February, which translated from the Old to New Style calendars becomes

Wooden image of Gobnait.

Kilsarkan Church, County Kerry.

The Castlemagner figure.

1st February and identical, therefore, with the Feast Day of Saint Brigit.

At the medieval parish church of Kilsarkan in County Kerry, a sheela-na-gig is also carved into the lintel of the window, and a major part of the traditional rounds is to rub the figure with a stone or pebble. This also includes rubbing in a cross pattern on several places around the whole window frame and on the stone sill.

Flanking the doorway of Saint Brigit's Well at Castlemagner in County Cork is a curious and rather rotund figure with upraised arms that may be closely related to the sheela-na-gig tradition, as it appears to be naked and possibly female. However, like the sheela-na-gigs, the figure has been rubbed with pebbles or stones in a cross pattern on her head, belly, and thighs. Andersen published two photographs of this figure taken some thirty-five years apart, showing considerable wear and spreading of the rubbed area over a relatively short period. A carved image that can be more clearly defined as a sheela-na-gig was found lying beside a holy well at Castlewidenham, also in County Cork, and this is recorded as being frequently rubbed for help in childbirth.

The Seir Kieran figure.

According to local knowledge, the two sheela-na-gigs at Kiltinane were said to represent an ancient fertility goddess, and accordingly, barren women would scrape the figure on the church for its healing dust. When James O'Connor studied photographs of the figure before carving a replica of the Kiltinane church's sheela-na-gig, he became convinced that the triangular area just below the genitals could not possibly have been the work of the original stonecutter and deduced that it must have been scraped out over time.

Probably the most fascinating example of a rubbed sheela-na-gig yet discovered is the remarkable figure that was built into the church at Seir Kieran in County Offaly. It is carved in deep relief and is depicted as seated, touching its genital area with one hand and holding some cylindrical object in the other. However, it is difficult to define exactly what represents the genitals, as there are so many deep holes are drilled into the figure. A large one between its feet may represent the vulva, but there are seven in its abdomen, plus one located in its throat and a further two more in the top of its head.

Evidence of rubbing can be inferred from the smoothness of some of the holes, especially the lowest, but one can only speculate on their purpose. Allusions have been made to the possible connection between these holes and the so-called cup marks found on megalithic stones as well as the basin stones known as bullaun stones found at both prehistoric and early Christian sites. Many of these old stones still form the focus of traditional devotion at ancient sites around the country, and like the vulvae of the sheela-na-gigs, there is a belief in them as symbols of fertility.

Christianity as it had evolved in Ireland up until the medieval period was fundamentally an insular development, uniquely blended with the strong Gaelic/Celtic tradition and structured upon the native cultural systems. Through the Early Christian period and right up to the final cultural genocide of the historical era, Ireland largely retained its ancient social structure, the pattern of kinship, and bardic or druidic traditions with its history of learning, poetry, and storytelling.

In the beginning, there was a very smooth assimilation of the new religion and the old order, but the arrival of the Roman orders, exemplified with the myths of Saint Patrick in the sixth century, heralded an era of deep conflict between the original Early Christian structure and the newer Roman version. This conflict is supposed to have ended with the coming of the Normans, but by the Middle Ages, they had been assimilated to such an extent that they actually instigated a period of Gaelic/Celtic revival.

Given such a context, it is not possible to simply categorize the sheela-na-gigs as either a Christian demon or a pagan idol, but rather, they represent a merging and blending of Christian and pagan ways. This blend of pagan and Christian is certainly not confined to the sheela-na-gigs, as there are many carved stones from the Early Christian period both in Ireland and Britain with designs and symbols that appear to bear little relation to the Christian tradition as we generally perceive it.

While the Christian God was superficially accepted, the Irish people continued their belief in the superiority of the feminine deities, as expressed through their local native goddesses and sacred spiritual women-turned-saints, in whose legends we have a conflation of Christian and pagan elements.

"Saint" Brigit is the clearest example of the transition of a pagan goddess into Christian saint, and there can be no doubt that she spans the two worlds of pagan and Christian tradition. Miranda Green suggested that Brigit personifies the old pagan Earth Mother Goddess in her most persistent form, while Mary Conderen, author of *The Goddess and the Serpent*, described the sheela-na-gig placed above the doorway of Killinaboy Church as an image of Brigit being placed there to "allow the congregation to enter the church through her womb." In making such a comparison, Conderen is well aware of the fact that the sheela-na-gig at Killinaboy occupies exactly the same position as the Virgin Mary on Catholic churches of the more modern era. Although the sheela-na-gig and the later sanitized Roman model of a saintly figure are incompatible images, the perception of sanctity was most likely very different to those earthier people of the Middle Ages who built the church.

In the ancient Irish world, Brigit was the daughter of the Dagdha, the "Good God," the patron of poetry, smithing, the seers, and the healing arts. Into Christian times, Brigit can be seen as carrying on her father's legacy with virtually all of his attributes being transferred to her. It has been suggested that Brigit is a title rather than a personal name, as it derives from the Celtic word *bríg* or *bríog*, which means "high one" or "exalted one." While many of the old Irish Goddesses were tied to particular places and intimately identified with the land, Brigit was a transportable goddess who transcended territorial consideration and was worshipped in many parts of Britain, Gaul, and as far away as Scandinavia, as numerous dedications to her attest. It is no wonder that Christianity quickly enlisted her into their hierarchy and turned her into a primary saint who was honored equally with Saint Patrick. In the Christian mythology the saint Brigit is said to have lived in the fifth century A.D., but she is easily recognizable as being the same person as the earlier goddess Brigit. Even her biographers describe her in ways that enhance her former status in the pagan world.

One example of this is the way she is woven into the story of the Battle of Moytura, the final battle between the Fomorians and the Tuatha DeDánann for the possession of Ireland, where Brigit appears as a mediator, an ancestor-deity, and a mother goddess whose main concern was the future well-being of Ireland. As a baby, the pagan Brigit is fed on the milk of a white, red-eared, otherworldly cow, and flames rise from her head. The pagan fire festival of Imbolc, marking the beginning of spring and celebrated in her honor, was retained and renamed Saint Brigit's Day. On this day, crosses made of rushes are still placed on buildings to guard against evil spirits, and the survival of such pagan associations show how it was the deliberate policy of the church to take over the symbols of the old religion and to convert them to Christian use.

As the "virgin mother" Mary ascended to her exalted position in the church of Europe during the Middle Ages, so too did the image of Brigit in Ireland, who became known as the Mary of the Gaels. References to her being called the "mother of the High King of Heaven" suggest that her role was nearly identical to that of Mary's. Even their feast days are almost identical, with the purification of the blessed Virgin Mary falling on February 2nd, the day after Brigit's feast day. It is a remarkable fact that in her conversion to Christianity, Brigit became even more powerful: a singular goddess rising above all former goddesses in synchronicity with the development of an increasingly monotheistic Christianity.

Those mysterious female figures of Inghean Bhoaithe and Gobnait, despite being highly venerated, are unofficial saints whose place in church history is uncertain, enduring only through the common people's devotion to them and the mythology surrounding them. In Gobnait, we are looking at a goddess of very ancient origin. Her association with bees—the symbol of life, death, and regeneration in both pagan and Christian times—has invested her with all the attributes of the old goddesses and indissolubly connected to all those older forms of devotion.

In Britain, there is also evidence to suggest that paganism was not immediately suppressed by Christianity. In 1282, the priest at Inverkeithing in Fife had to appear before his bishop for leading a fertility dance at Easter around a phallic figure, and in the fourteenth century, the Bishop of Exeter was shocked to learn that the monks of Frithelstock Priory in Devon "were wont to worship a statue like the unchaste Diana at an altar in the woods"—hiding their sheela-na-gig away from the church authorities, perhaps.

Carvings such as the green man, with its obvious pagan overtones, were erected throughout Britain at the same time that the sheela-na-gigs were being put on the churches, and professor and data scientist Geoffrey Webb has found phallic symbols concealed inside the altars of almost 90% of medieval churches built up until the time of the Black Death. Many of the pagan elements that made up the earlier church were systematically withdrawn or hidden away, as the church progressed into the era of the Renaissance, and the sheela-na-gigs would most certainly be among those elements that were less easily assimilated into the church.

THE LIVING SHEELA-NA-GIGS

Barbara Freitag revealed many instances of traditions that add to our understanding of the place of the sheela-na-gigs within a traditional culture, and she recognized the need to concentrate research on the folklore that relates to them. Although valid in relation to the sheela-na-gigs, most of these references relate to traditions about wise and holy women and less specifically about the actual figures themselves. Among the references she unearthed, some relate to a festival, once very widespread, which was held the day after Saint Patrick's Day and known as "Sheela's Day," Sheela being the wife of Patrick. This tradition died out around the time that the sheela-na-gigs were being recognized by antiquarians in the mid-1800s and appears to have been severely discouraged by the church authorities of the time.

According to the account of the German researcher Johann Kohl, who traveled around Ireland at around the time the sheela-na-gigs were first being recognized by O'Donovan and Coles, the figures had something to do with an ancient custom of averting ill luck or evil. A man afflicted by bad luck might turn for help to a certain class of women known as "Shila na Gigh," who would display themselves in order to avert evil and bring about good luck. In the

1930s, when Edith Guest was researching in the Macroom area of County Cork, a middle-aged woman did not understand the sense in which she was using the word and "derived some puzzled comment from it, wondering why I should desire to seek out old women of the type which I may for brevity describe as a hag." According to Johann Kohl, the living sheela-na-gigs were probably the same women known also as the gieradors, who, according to the seventeenth-century Kilmore Diocesan Synod, were banned from receiving the sacraments. The word *gierador* apparently refers to a woman who turned the evil eye, the fortune teller or diviner, the local hag or witch. Like the name sheela-na-gig, gierador may be a local colloquialism.

The practice of displaying the genitalia as a means of opposing evil or of slighting enemies is a practice that is well attested to in Ireland. In a letter to the Irish Times from September 23rd, 1977, Walter Mahon-Smith gives a personal testimony of how in 1913, a bloody faction fight was averted: "In a townland near where I lived, a deadly feud had continued for generations between the families of two small farmers. One day, before the first World War, when the men of one of the families, armed with pitchforks and heavy blackthorn sticks, attacked the home of their enemy, the woman-of-the-house came to the door of her cottage, and in full sight of all (including my father and myself who happened to be passing by), lifted her skirt and underclothes high above her head, displaying her naked genitals. The enemy of her and her family fled in terror."

The nineteenth-century researcher Windele noted in relation to a sheela-na-gig at Barnahealy in Cork that "they are called Hags of the Castle, and when placed above the key stone of the door arch were supposed to possess a tutelary or protective power so that an enemy passing by would be disarmed of evil intent against the building upon seeing it." Such statements suggest that the figures were regarded as being invested with great power, and a few of the figures such as the sheela-na-gig from Carrick Castle in Kildare and the so-called Cat Goddess with entwined legs (once regarded as a sheela-na-gig) on the Rock of Cashel were both called the "Evil Eye Stone." Both the Barnahealy and Carrick Castle sheela-na-gigs have since gone missing.

Another missing sheela-na-gig formerly on Ballynamona Castle was damaged by someone offended by it, and a later search for the figure around the turn of the century found her some distance away but so smashed up that she was beyond repair. A report of this figure states that "It is certain that once she left her place in the castle, the Nagles [who built the castle] did not long survive her."

Barbara Freitag has published a considerable store of references from folklore records that shed light on the traditions and stories that relate to sacred women, female healers, and the belief in the many female deities who were said to inhabit the visible world. From this, it is possible to form a picture of a world that is not so long gone, in which those women who practiced skills such as healing and midwifery were held in high regard. As such, the few references to objects that appear likely to have been sheela-na-gigs were invariably written of most respectfully, as befits an image that reflects the power of the feminine in its most sacred form.

THE GNOSTIC CONNECTION

Over three decades ago, the filmmaker and writer Bob Quinn suggested a connection between the sheela-na-gigs and Coptic Gnosticism. In his ground-breaking TV series called *Atlantean*, first aired on the Irish National Broadcasting channel RTE in the 1980s, he suggested a connection between early Chris-

The Taughboy Sheela-na-gig.

tianity and the appearance of the sheela-na-gigs. Conventional dating places the sheela-na-gigs in the period much later than the Early Christian era, and the film was released at the time when the theory that the Normans introduced them as an anti-sex image was becoming the ruling dogma, so it is not surprising that his ideas were largely ignored. A Gnostic/Coptic origin for the sheela-na-gigs would, however, resolve several questions regarding certain aspects of the figures and the context in which many of them are found.

The one sheela-na-gig that hints at more going on than meets the historian's eye is the figure that was revealed when ivy was removed from the western gable of Taughboy Church in Roscommon. This is the only known example of a sheela-na-gig being erected at the very apex of a church wall, where it requires a telescopic lens to be seen in detail. In such a position, it is much more hidden than almost all of the rest of the sheela-na-gigs, as if she is hiding in plain sight.

This sheela-na-gig is depicted in squatting posture, and an unusual aspect is the bulbous feature that perhaps depicts a clitoris within the cleft of the vulva. Most curious of all is a strange extension below the vulva that might represent the flow of water but, after a good deal of scrutiny, appears much more like a phallus. Is it not possible that this sheela-na-gig might represent evidence of a Gnostic sex magic type of tradition being followed in this once quite remote monastic center at some time in the mysterious past?

Taughboy Church is all that is left of a former monastic center and it is situated in an area of County Roscommon where all five of the county's sheela-na-gigs are clustered. The closest sheela-na-gig to this one is on Cloghan Castle, less than 1.5 kilometers to the north, which also has a curious protrusion extending below the vulva.

CHAPTER FOUR

THE NORMAN/IRISH AND THE HAG OF THE CASTLE

IN ITS ORIGINAL FORM, the sheela-na-gig was a religious motif, and almost all of the figures in Britain and Europe are found on churches or other religious structures dating from the Romanesque period. In Ireland, however, there was a continued development of the image during the following three centuries and an expansion of their use on castles and other secular structures. About half of the known sheela-na-gigs were erected on castles or other non-religious structures, and most of the known Irish figures date to the later medieval/Middle Ages period—from the 1300s to the end of the Gaelic culture in the 1600s.

In this era, they became a totemic icon signifying a particularly special deity or figure related to the family or clan of the structures upon which they were placed—something that is almost entirely unique to Ireland and the main reason why this island contains by far the greatest quantity of sheela-na-gigs.

The fact that they appear on the castles is one of the most integral elements of the story of these extraordinary figures, as it emphasizes how much the culture of the period embraced this image and forces us to take a fresh look into the later medieval world that created them. The sheela-na-gigs we find on those old clan castles obviously represented an essential iconic element to the people who put them there and, as such, are a poignant reminder of just how little we know about the world that created them.

The most important fact about this period in Irish history is that it was a period of Gaelic/Celtic cultural resurgence—a time in which the old Gaelic traditions were being re-established and re-invigorated. This is the main key to an understanding of

Ballinderry Castle, main entrance door.

the figures. Instead of thinking of the Middle Ages in Ireland as a war-torn era dominated by the English and Normans, we need to see that the reality is that it was an era in which those apparently competing forces were, in fact, interacting within society, often on an equal basis, and equally anxious to establish their identities within that society. In this world, the widespread use of the sheela-na-gig image on churches and castles was an essential part of this search for identity.

Some of the sheela-na-gigs found on castles were locally believed to have originated from churches. Of course, there is no certain way of knowing the original site or age of any carved stone, but it is generally thought that most of the castle figures appear to have been created specifically for the building on which they are found.

The Sheela-na-gig above the door of Ballinderry Castle.

Ballyfinboy Castle.

The medieval culture, which is responsible for the widespread appearance of the "Hag of the Castle," a name by which the figures are often known, has its roots in the Norman invasion of 1169. According to the most widely disseminated versions of history, this event supposedly cut the knot of the Irish dynastic or kinship system and allowed for the establishment of a feudal structure based on the continental model. History, as usual, and especially in Ireland, is not that simple, however.

While the main political motive of both the English monarchy and the papacy was the restructuring of the Irish political and religious system, the adventuring Norman barons who undertook this war were, of course, anxious to gain secure positions in Irish society as well as new lands. But even in the process of achieving their aims, these invaders were rapidly merging into the Irish culture, and their integration into the Irish septs and clans formed an integral part of the process of settling into their new territories.

In outward appearance, the society that developed after this period was greatly influenced by the new ideas brought by the Normans. Yet the speed of their assimilation into Irish culture has often been remarked upon. Irish and

Normans intermarried freely, mingled freely, and entered readily into alliances, so that within a hundred years after their arrival in Ireland, many of the Norman barons were the grandsons of twelfth-century Irish kings, and many of the later Irish kings were the grandsons of thir-teenth-century Normans.

Patrick Wallace, former curator of the National Museum of Ireland, has pointed out that within fifty years of the Norman invasion, the man elected as chief Bre-hon of Ireland (the equivalent of attor-ney general) was a direct descendant of a Norman lord. Just who, then, were these Normans, if one of the could rise to the head of the country's native law system in such a short period of time?

Sheela-na-gig from Blackhall Castle, Kildare.

The name *Norman* stems from their origins as men from the North, Norse-men, or the Vikings, who were given a large tract of land known as Neustria as a gift for not entirely slaughtering all the Christians in Europe in the tenth century. The word *Norman* existed long before they took over northern France; among others, the historian Bede (the "venerable Bede") used the term Nor-mans two centuries before the establishment of the Normans in Normandy. As lords of Neustria, these Vikings became the mercenaries of Rome, the military arm of the church and French monarchy who could be brought in to quell any thoughts of rebellion against Rome.

At first, the Vikings/Normans fought battles against the Bretons and other opponents of the French monarchy. Then in 1066, they marched into England, and a century later, into Ireland. But behind the usual historical points of refer-ence in their history, they had deep connections with the Gaelic/Celtic world, which had its roots in Viking days. Although much desired by Rome, the Nor-man invasion of Ireland was only possible after it had been activated through their ancestral connections with the island and involvement with its internal

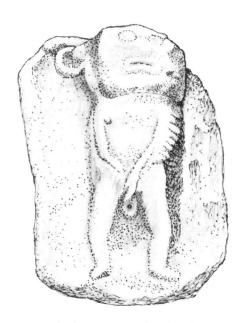

Sheela-na-gig on Redwood Castle,
the MacEgan bardic school.

power struggles. The Normans who invaded Ireland therefore would have had a very good knowledge of the ways of Ireland, its social structures, and the way power operated.

Consequently, the assimilation of the Normans into Irish society was largely engineered through negotiation and in accordance with a certain deference to the system already operating within Gaelic society. The day-to-day work of establishing themselves in Ireland depended mostly on developing their Irish connections, and among the higher classes, this was often achieved through that most ancient of social systems: by marrying into the ruling Irish families.

As soon as the Normans started to inhabit Ireland, a system was soon developed to allow mediation between the Irish and the Norman/English that took account of both law structures. Sir William Wilde pointed out that in order to conciliate the Irish, the Norman DeBurgo family of the west shook off obedience to the English law and renounced their allegiance to the English crown. Within a century of their arrival in Ireland, they had adopted Irish both in dress and language and changed their names to Bourke or Burke, a common name today in the west of Ireland. A similar transition occurred throughout the country so that by the fourteenth century, assimilation of the Normans into Irish life was the norm.

Thus the world of the Middle Ages in Ireland was fashioned within a structure based on both the old Gaelic/Celtic Brehon system and that of Britain and the Roman church. In The Templars, the Witch, and the Wild Irish, a groundbreaking study of the heresy trials of the Middle Ages, Maeve Brigid Callan quotes a statute issued in Kilkenny in 1366 that warns about the many English

(Anglo-Normans) who have forsaken the English language and fashions, and govern themselves in accordance with Irish laws and customs. Most worrisome to the English colonial authorities were the marriages and alliances with the native Irish, which sometimes elevated their status above those of the English. This was the situation in the eastern "pale," a region almost entirely dominated by the English, so it can be assumed that the Norman/English in the west would have assimilated to an even greater degree.

In the fourteenth century, special bardic families were chosen to act as advisors to the ruling Irish/Norman chiefs, and this system actually expanded during the Middle Ages after a number of the Norman/English families ran into difficulties and their land was returned to the Gaelic tenants. One of the chief bardic families of the western Midlands region, the MacEgans, had a bardic school in their castle at Redwood on the Shannon, which incidentally has a sheela-na-gig above the doorway.

The Anglo/Norman lords not only carried on the tradition of patronage toward the religious foundations, as the Irish chiefs had done before them, but as the many ruined monasteries and abbeys still to be seen around the country testify, the Middle Ages was also a period of unprecedented expansion and development of the monastic system.

Investment in the monasteries was not purely for religious purposes, as those establishments were the very center—the hub of culture and learning at the time, from their houses of hospitality and healing (from whence we get the word hospital) to their great libraries and scriptoriums. It should be noted, particularly when trying to understand the sheela-na-gigs, that it was these monastic centers and their patrons the old Gaelic/Norman lords who bequeathed to us the most extensive record of lore, mythology, and ancient history in the Western world. This can be considered proof that they regarded such things with the utmost sincerity.

Despite the historical perspective of an unstable land riven by war, the Middle Ages was actually a time of relative abundance, the wealth of the country being one of the main reasons it was targeted so ruthlessly by the British in the sixteenth and seventeenth centuries. Evidence of the prosperity of the land at this time can be seen in the many castles still standing on the landscape, which date from the same era that the sheela-na-gigs saw their height in popularity.

Sheela-na-gig on Ballinacarriga Castle.

Apart from the practical purposes of storage and defense, the castles of the later medieval period are analogous to the earlier medieval churches as centers of the community, and as such, many were adorned with religious motifs traditionally reserved for the religious houses. A good example of this is Ballinacarriga Castle in County Cork, a well-preserved late sixteenth-century tower house that is an eligible reminder of both the standing of the Gaelicised Norman clans of the time and the regard with which such structures were often held. The main floor, which can be reached by climbing the intact staircase to the top, was used as a chapel or church until its eventual demise in the mid-1800s, and it is particularly noted for its many fine carvings, nearly all of a religious nature.

One of the carvings is of a woman depicted carrying an emblem of the triple deity, thought to be Catherine Cullinane (Collins). Despite that it is known generally as Randolf Hurley's castle, it is to his wife Catherine that the castle is dedicated, and on its eastern wall is one of the finest sheela-na-gigs in the region.

But it was not out of just sentimentality that we see Catherine being honored, for it is recorded that the title deeds to the castle were in the hands of a woman, Ellen Randall (née de Courcey), during the 1600s, so it would appear that a matriarchal inheritance may have been a traditional aspect of the tenure of these lands. This shows that theirs was a marriage based on the ancient Brehon law structure, whereby women were often the traditional heirs to the land. This is a typical, although better illustrated than usual, example of the type of intermarriage between clans that personified the era. Such marriages were common all through the Middle Ages.

The widespread occurrence of sheela-na-gigs on castles can be seen as an extension of that same religious intent that caused them to be placed on the churches in the first place, especially considering that they were still being erected on churches during this later period. In certain instances, the castle had a similar social standing or function as the church, and the erection of the sheela-na-gigs represents another example of the prominent place that religion held in the lives of those people. Sheela-na-gigs were not the only import of church ornaments, for these castles also employed that motif perhaps most closely allied to them: the human head, which is also considered to have had an apotropaic function.

The influence of the Gaelic revival is clearly visible in a number of the better-preserved castles that still retain some portion of their highly decorated lintels, window bosses, door surrounds, and numerous other carvings in which there is a liberal use of Celtic-style artwork. This prevailing attitude of cultural revivalism is exemplified in the figure carved onto a keystone over the main entrance to Ballinderry Castle in County Galway: a well-preserved late tower house, traditionally the last of the castles built in the area. The image of the sheela-na-gig here is set within a framework that contains knotwork patterns, a triskelion, a marigold or sun symbol, and other important Celtic motifs.

Another excellent and closely related example, also carved on a keystone, was found buried in the graveyard at Rahara Church, about forty kilometers east of Ballinderry. This figure, which now safely resides in Roscommon County Museum, was until recently the only other sheela-na-gig depicted with associated Celtic patterns, and the image here is simpler than at Ballinderry being set within a frame of knotwork. The most recent discovery of a third figure with associated Celtic patterning is actually located about midway between Ballinderry Castle and the old church at Rahara, over the border in Roscommon, and suggests a connection between the three figures. We may indeed be looking at the hand of a single carver. The original location of the Clootymurraghy figure is not known, and it is currently in private ownership on a remote farm in eastern County Galway.

It is noticeable that the greatest density of sheela-na-gigs from this later period can be found around the areas of very rich land or areas of political and religious importance, such as around Cashel in County Tipperary and around the River Shannon. These lands lay chiefly in the areas of Norman influence and settlement, and the spread of the use of the motif almost certainly appears to be attributable to the cultural assimilation of the Norman/Irish in an area where a large amount of castle and church building was going on.

Sheela-na-gigs erected during this later period are often larger and more eccentric than ever before, and although the genitals are well defined, they appear to depend less exclusively upon their sex. Andersen suggested that this is a more aggressive type of figure with broad, heavy shoulders becoming a consistent feature, in keeping with the development of a militaristic castle-building culture. Yet the idol-like effect of the heavy-shouldered sheela-na-gig is not a new stylization; it is evident in some of the earliest figures, such as those from churches at Seir Kieran, Errigal Keeroge, and Lavey. This powerful frontality is also evident in the figure on Saint Adamnan's Pillar at Tara, and is even better illustrated in that most heavily built and also possibly very early sheela-na-gig or sheela-like figure that looms out of a standing stone erected over a little spring near the old monastic settlement at Stepaside near Dublin.

A feature unique to the castle sheela-na-gigs is the broad, open posture with feet touching the edge of the stone, as can be seen on the formidable hags, such as those at Dunnaman, Croomantagh, Tullovin, and Ballyfinboy. Even the later, more simplified sheela-na-gig on a quoin from Clenagh Castle retains the aspect of her feet turned out to touch the edge of the quoin. In this aspect, the feet themselves are often exaggerated, sometimes with highly stylized toes, which may symbolize their earthly nature, or possibly emphasizes the point of contact with the material world. Sheela-na-gigs with their feet touching the edge of the stone are also found on churches, although they are by no means as powerful-looking.

The tradition that's attached to these castle sheela-na-gigs suggests a strong belief in their apotropaic or talismanic function, which may simply be an extension of their original function on churches. One of the earliest references to this is by the antiquarian researcher John Windele who, in the 1850s, reported on a figure found at Barnahealy, County Cork: "This is one of those old Fetish figures often found in Ireland on the fronts of churches as well as Castles, they are called Hags of the Castle and when placed above the key stone of the door arch were supposed to possess a tutelary or protective power so that an enemy passing by would be disarmed of evil intent against the building on seeing it."

An apotropaic function attributed to the medieval castle sheela-na-gigs would lead one to expect that they would be placed in more prominent situations than they actually are. Certainly, there are figures like that on the castle of Dunaman in Limerick, which have been erected directly facing the main entrance. The majority were located high up on the external castle wall, and though

The broad posture of Dunnaman Sheela-na-gig.

they are never hidden or out of sight, very few are found in places that would be immediately viewed by those approaching the castle. One example of this is the figure on Ballinacarriga Castle, for although it is quite a large and clearly delineated figure, it is situated at a height of about ten meters on the wall above the main entrance and is seldom noticed unless specifically pointed out. Similarly at Redwood Castle in Tipperary, the sheela-na-gig is barely visible, being tucked away under an overhanging barbican about twelve meters above the main entrance doorway.

Those sheela-na-gigs on quoins might give us a better clue to their function, since they are carved on a specifically designed stone that renders a fundamentally supportive role in the structure of the building. A magical role has been suggested for the quoin stones, but in any case, it is easy to appreciate that these carefully worked and specifically keyed-in stones would be regarded as being in an auspicious position for a protective totem such as a sheela-na-gig.

The curious 'four-eyed' Taghmon figure above a trefoil window.

Figures carved on quoin stones are similarly found high up on the walls of castles and are often not easy to see. The sheela-na-gigs on the castles of Tullovin, Croomantagh, Ballaghmore, and Cloghan are all very high up, and though clearly visible, they do not constitute a pronounced feature. Meanwhile, the figure on Doon Castle is set on a quoin only a little higher than the entrance door, and the figure on Clenagh Castle is exceptionally low to the ground. The carving of sheela-na-gigs on quoin stones was not entirely restricted to castles, as those at Kiltinane and Malahide were set as quoins, and the figure thought to have come from Lavey Church appears as if it was also a quoin. These churches date to roughly the same period as the tower houses, and in the cases of Kiltinane and Malahide, the quoin stone is situated immediately below the roof at the springing of the gable: a vulnerable point from which the roof would once have risen. In Britain, there are only two definite sheela-na-gigs that were used as quoin stones: on the churches of Fiddington and Pennington, both of which are places of former Gaelic/Celtic influence. That there are more sheela-na-gigs set as quoins on castles is possibly merely because of the endurance of castles, as compared to the more vulnerable churches.

John Feehan has noted the possibility of sheela-na-gigs found on castles being regarded as protectors of a border, though he went a little too far in his suggestion that "they only occur on border castles." He cites the example of two figures on the castles of Cullahill and Ballaghmore in County Offaly, which were both built in the fifteenth century by the Gaelic chieftain Mac

Tullovin.

Giolla Phádraig (Fitzpatrick), the Lord of Upper Ossory. Strategically placed as they were on the old Irish Road, they were the main defenders of the province of Munster to the south and Leinster to the north. These figures are situated near the southern and northern boundaries of their territory facing out toward the border, and they are the only sheela-na-gigs that can still be found on any of the Fitzpatricks' castles.

An apotropaic function in guarding the approach or entrance to the town is clearly a feature of the three sheela-na-gigs from Fethard, Thurles, and Drogheda that are found on town walls in areas of Norman settlement. The figure from Fethard is on a section of the fourteenth-century town wall, overlooking the old medieval bridge over the Clashawley River and strategically located facing the old entrance into the town. Curiously, just like the castle sheela-na-gigs erected high up on the wall, this fearsome figure is difficult to make out from a distance and is indistinguishable from the wall—that is, until one has actually crossed over the bridge, and then one is faced by perhaps one of the scariest-looking figures of the whole genre.

At Taghmon, a very odd, four-eyed, heavy-shouldered figure is situated

Sheela na Guira.

over a trefoil window in the north wall of the semi-fortified manorial fifteenth-century church. This figure is a little ambiguous, but a hole where the vulva is usually situated shows that it is carved in the tradition of the sheela-na-gigs. The present church has a stone arched roof, and an addition of a four-story tower makes the building look more like a castle than a church. The strong emphasis on security due to regular inter-tribal fighting suggests that, in this respect, the sheela-na-gig is a protective icon that would be fundamental in guarding the house of the spirit.

The two sheela-na-gigs from Round Towers are also situated on or close to windows. The figure in the round tower at Ratoo, the only sheela-na-gig so far identified on a round tower, is situated on the top left-hand corner of the north window, and the now-detached figure at Toomregan is thought to have formed the lintel of a narrow, splayed, round-headed window of a round tower. Likewise, the figures from the churches at Kilsarkan, Ballyvourney, Cashel, and Rathblathmaic have been erected above or in the vicinity of windows, often forming part of the lintel. In comparison there is very little association with sheela-na-gigs and the windows of castles, the only example being found on the inner reveal of a window at the top of the southwestern tower at Bunratty Castle, although this is not thought to be its original position. Undoubtedly, windows are not such a prominent feature of castles and, as such, probably did not need additional protection.

There are other instances suggesting that the sheela-na-gigs were placed on castles as clan totems and that they may have represented a deity or entity peculiar to that clan or family. For instance, the figure from Cullahill Castle in

County Laois was known as Sheela na Guira, which was locally translated as Gillian O'Dwyer, head of the O'Gara clan and said to be a "bit of a tyrant." The sheela-na-gig that formerly adorned the south wall of the castle at Moycarkey is now known only from a sketch in the Royal Irish Academy which bears the caption "The country people have a legend and call it Cathleen Owen," which relates to her as a river hag like "the 'washer at the ford.'" (*Owen* means "river" in Irish.) Another example is the figure formerly at Corveen in Donegal, where the sheela-na-gig is known to have originated from a castle on the original island fortress on Lough Eske. This was the island stronghold of the O'Donnells, the ruling clan of Tireconnel, Donegal, and it was obviously an important enough clan emblem that it was subsequently removed to the new castle that was built on the mainland (although it then went missing).

The erection of sheela-na-gigs on castles appears to be merely an extension of their religious context, and the evidence suggests that their function was nothing other than a more overt expression of their previous one. There is no doubt that a more extravagant symbolism is being employed in the figures that were erected on castles, which could have been because of the ancient beliefs being resuscitated at the time concerning the spiritual elements residing in the land and the power of the figures to ward off evil.

While it appears that the later figures had a powerful apotropaic function and possibly also acted as clan totems, there is little association with any fertility function, let alone any association with representing "anti-lust." Indeed, it seems very odd that these figures were erected on castles at all if they were not taking on some sort of positive role or function. It is also evident that the Normans played a large role that contributed to not only a massive campaign of castle-building, but also helped to initiate a period of Gaelic/Celtic revivalism that resulted in doubling the number of sheela-na-gigs in Ireland.

The sheela-na-gig as an image representing the spiritual guardian of the land could also be seen as an example of the Gaelic/Celtic people's desire to establish themselves as rightful stewards of the lands.

While the Normans may have significantly contributed to the spread of the sheela-na-gigs, it is going a little too far to suggest that the earlier twelfth- and thirteenth-century figures were introduced into England and Ireland by the Normans, who imported the motif as a continuation of their continental tradition of carving humanoid figures.

Had the carving of sheela-na-gigs been a common tradition originating on the continent, one might suspect that the earlier wave of Normans who established themselves in England a century before they landed in Ireland, and who had closer ties with their former continental homelands, would have carried on this native tradition on their British castles. Yet this was not the case, for the tradition of putting sheela-na-gigs on castles is entirely an Irish phenomenon.

A Norman origin for the sheela-na-gigs also fails to account for the fact that they are found both prior to, and outside of, areas influenced by the Normans. Moreover, the Normans are mainly credited with introducing English Gothic art and architecture to Ireland, but not the Romanesque style, which was being superseded by Gothic architecture by the time the Normans were establishing themselves in Ireland. Evidence to suggest that the Normans imported the exhibitionist motif from the continent appears quite insubstantial. But whether or not they were the vehicle through which the motif traveled to Ireland, it is certain that once it arrived on Irish soil, it followed the same pattern as the Normans themselves: becoming thoroughly ingrained into Irish culture in a very short space of time and ending up as a unique product of the culture of Ireland and the idiosyncratic Irish imagination.

CHAPTER FIVE

THE MYTHOLOGY
OF THE SHEELA-NA-GIGS

A CENTRALLY IMPORTANT CHARACTER in many of the mythological stories, particularly those relating to sovereignty, death, or warfare, was a fearsome and sometimes grotesque supernatural female deity known as the hag or crone, the cailleach, or sometimes as the banshee. Descriptions of the various hags or crones vary widely, but there is a remarkable similarity between them and the features that we find on the sheela-na-gigs. These spirit beings that the mythic heroes encounter usually have either an otherworldly look or a fierce countenance, and they often appear in the various magical postures: aspects that are represented among the sheela-na-gigs.

Typically the hag is described as an old woman with a bald head, cadaverous ribs, sagging abdomen, and small breasts, which is virtually identical to the general description of many of the sheela-na-gigs. It seems quite clear then that many are, at least in part, modeled on the descriptions of these powerful female figures.

In mythology, superior magical abilities, especially that of prophetic vision, are usually attributed to a female shaman, and there are many references to *banfhilí*, women who practice special rituals to acquire *imbas forosnai*, a gift of that vision. These spiritual women form a very important part of the legendary stories built up around such figures as the messianic Sétanta (bet-

St. Adamnan's Pillar, Tara, with its Sheela-na-gig.

ter known as Cúchulainn) and Fionn Mac Cumhaill (sometimes anglicized as Finn McCool), where they act in both a guiding role and a teaching role. To the ancients, the vision was greater than something of a purely material nature, and it is hardly coincidental that even these mythic heroes are shown as subordinate to the power of these elemental spirits of the land.

The hag is fundamentally an earth goddess and a tutelary sovereign, responsible for the fortunes, fertility, and prosperity of her territory. This was such a primary aspect of ancient belief that the rulers of the land married their tutelary goddess in a ritual known as the Ban Fis. The best-known examples of this ritual relate to sites such as Tara, the coronation site of the High King of Ireland, but it was a ritual enacted at all of the inauguration centers, including those of the lesser clan chiefs throughout the country.

In Ireland, this tradition of tribal kingship and the rite of sacral marriage to the goddess of the land was of huge importance and is reflected in the old Brehon law system, whereby the land was often handed down through a female line—a tradition that was largely destroyed after the collapse of traditional Irish Gaelic culture in the 1600s.

The inauguration involved several further ordeals that tested the candidate's fitness as king. At Tara, the Lia Fáil, a phallic stone situated on the Hill of Tara, was said to cry out if the man who presented himself to be king was not the rightful heir to the position. A pair of stones, currently standing near the present-day church, are known as the Blocc and Bluigne. Standing but a hand's breadth apart, they served to test whether a man was the rightful king. If he was, the stones would open wide enough to give passage to the man and his chariot, which symbolizes the opening of the legs to allow the king entry to the sacred precinct. One of these two stones is quite low and squat, and the other is a narrow vertical stone known as Saint Adamnan's Pillar. Significantly, into this second stone is carved a sheela-na-gig.

The hag's association with life, fertility, and death is symbolized by her ability to shape-shift between three forms: a beautiful maiden, a powerful sexual woman, and an old woman or crone. The theme of an ancient hag wandering the countryside, ugly and unkempt, recurs throughout many of the old stories. In most tales, she transforms into a beautiful young woman upon meeting and mating with a man who is destined to become the rightful king. But in others, where the man was not suitable for kingship, the hag did not transform, and she brought about his downfall.

The hag or cailleach is regularly related to water, and a common theme is the meeting of a hag who is washing clothes at a river, often referred to as the Washer at the Ford. She usually appears in connection with a final, fateful battle. A story that provides a glimpse into the realities of the medieval mind is the tale of the battle of Dysert O'Dea (O'Dea Castle), as recorded in *The Triumphs of Turlough*, a compilation of historical stories relating to County Clare. This battle took place in May of 1318 and is regarded as a crucial event, as it put an end to the Normans' hopes of conquering western Clare.

The story relates how the leader of the Normans, Richard de Clare, was leading his army when he came to a ford on the River Fergus. There, he saw a hag, "an horrific badb," who was washing clothes in the river, which ran red with blood. Through a translator, he asked whose clothes she was washing, and her reply was that they were his and that he would soon be dead. They were, of course, defeated. Close to where the battle took place is the ancient monastic site of Rathblathmaic, which overlooks a lake said to be inhabited by twenty-five banshees who washed the clothes of those doomed to die. A small, possibly very early image of a sheela-na-gig forms part of an ornate decorated panel inside the old church there. The banshee as the washer at the Ford was a theme that survived right up to the end of the old Gaelic/Celtic world: According to the bardic oral tradition, the last banshee was seen washing the clothes by the river at the Battle of Aughrim in 1691.

Sheela-na-gigs often have a close relationship with rivers or wells; several

The Sheela-na-gig as keystone above the door of Ballinderry Castle.

are found by sacred springs. That said, seeing as almost all of the churches or castles on which there are, or were, sheela-na-gigs are naturally situated close to a water source or a river, it is impossible to correlate their association through location. Several figures are of particular note, including the one known as Cathleen Owen (Catherine of the River) and the sheela-na-gig on the old wall at Fethard, which looks out at the nearby river. The unique figure on Ballinderry Castle in County Galway does as well. This sheela-na-gig appears to have some kind of fluid running from the vulva, and while most observers have suggested menstrual fluid, it is more likely to be a depiction of her as the goddess of the river: a water hag.

This sheela-na-gig may be representing Bóande, a goddess who appears in the origin myth of the Boyne Valley. The great mother goddess Bóande is described as standing with her legs apart over the river when she mates with the primary god, the Dagda. Such myths would have been well known by the people who lived in the castle at that time.

The banshee is still regarded as the death messenger of Irish tradition—the female spirit who is said to be heard to scream or cry, and on occasions be seen, at the time of a person's death. The terrifying wail of the banshee can be related to the goddess of war, Nemhain, of whom it is recorded that "when she raised her cry over the armies facing Cúchulainn, a hundred warriors of them fell dead that night of terror and fright."

The Sheela-na-gig formerly on Kiltinane Church.

In the saga "The Adventures of the Sons of Eochaid Mugmedon," Niall and his four brothers were out hunting when they were overcome by thirst. One of the brothers found a well, which was guarded over by a hideous hag, "bleary-eyed, fang-toothed, snotty-nosed, with a boil-encrusted body," who demanded a kiss in exchange for water. The first brother turned her down and fled in horror, and in turn, all of them reacted the same way, except for Niall. He responded to the hag's request by agreeing not only to kiss her but to sleep with her as well. As the two embraced, the hag was transformed into a lovely maiden, and Niall went on to accede to the throne.

Probably the most infamous goddess of war and harbinger of death was the Mórrígan, a trio of shape-shifting goddesses comprising Badb (meaning "battle crow"), Némain (meaning "frenzy"), or by Macha (meaning "plain"). Although these goddesses did not physically join in combat, their presence in a battle could encourage those whom they supported, and it foretold death for those they did not. Shortly before the battle of Mag Rath in 637 A.D., the Mórrígan appeared in the form of a lean, nimble hag, hovering and hopping about on the spears and shields of the army that was to be victorious.

Another instance of the war goddess in her guise as a hag occurs in the saga of "Togail Bruidne Dá Derga" (Da Derga's Hostel). The great king Conaire Mór is staying at the hostel and initially refuses entry to the hag, as he is under a geis (a curse or taboo) not to allow entry to a single woman after dark. The hag curses him, casting a baleful eye upon him, and foretells his death. Conaire Mór then asks the woman her name, and she chants him a list of her names while standing on one foot, holding one hand up, and breathing one breath. This list includes Badb and Némain, the names of war goddesses. The war goddess is described as a big woman with an evil eye, and this eye makes Conaire Mór think that she might be a seer. This is exactly the same one-legged and one-armed stance that is adopted by a number of sheela-na-gigs. Although Conaire Mór had already broken almost all of his taboos, the hag was the final omen of his impending death and doom: She ultimately forces him to break his final taboo by encouraging him to invite her to spend the night in the hostel.

The great mythic hero Cúchulainn is taunted by women and goddess figures throughout his life and always resists the pressure, until he finally meets his death through his fated encounter with three old crones as he heads toward his final battle. They are described as being blind in one eye and cooking dogs on spits while chanting spells. Cúchulainn's name means "the hound," and one of his taboos was that he was forbidden to eat the flesh of a dog, but the crones put such pressure on him that they force him to break this taboo. When he accepts some dog flesh, he is instantly weakened and then becomes easy prey for his final slaughter.

It is apparent that, at the time the sheela-na-gigs were being erected, there was a great belief in the power of female deities as protectors of the land, upon which the fertility and abundance on the land—and life and death in general—was dependent. The idea that warfare and fertility should be closely allied may seem a paradox at first, but more than likely, it reflects recognition that good and evil, giving and taking, and life and death are mutually interdependent. In the era of frequent inter-tribal fighting, the representation of goddesses of war was probably one of the most vivid ways of representing the goddess of death, who was just as intent on ensuring that what has come from the earth should return to it, in a form that will ensure its future fertility.

The goddess of sovereignty in her form as the hag represented a protector of the territories. If the land was to flourish and be productive, then the borders of the territory needed to be defended, and war may have been a necessary extension of the function of guardianship. The rulers and inhabitants of that land possessed the power of life and death, and embraced both war and sexuality in a manner that ensured general fertility. Sheela-na-gigs might have served an apotropaic function of protecting against evil, and this may also be an extension of their function of invoking prosperity and fertility.

Nakedness is one of the few features that all the sheela-na-gigs have in common, and there are significant references to the magical power of female nakedness in Irish mythology. In the story "The Intoxication of the Ultonians" (i.e., the men of Ulster), a female poet, Richis, wishes to avenge the death of her son killed in a battle with Cúchulainn, so she enlists the aid of another man to kill him. When Richis meets up with Cúchulainn, she takes off her clothes, and immediately Cúchulainn covers his face so that he might not see her nakedness. His charioteer warns him that a man is approaching to kill him, but Cúchulainn states that "whilst the woman is in that condition, shall I not rise up'." Seeing him magically subdued into inaction, the charioteer is forced to take matters into his own hands and throws a stone at Richis, which kills her and thus saves Cúchulainn's life.

The well-known "curse of the Ulster men" is a tale that relates how Macha, the tutelary goddess of Ulster, was forced to run a race against their champion horses while in the pangs of childbirth, and thereby cursed the men of Ulster. Accordingly, whenever they needed their power most, they would be overcome with pain like that felt by a woman in childbirth. Cúchulainn was absent from Macha's fateful race and was never afflicted with these pangs, as he probably averted his gaze. This eventually causes his death, as he is left alone on the final battlefield, the only one not doubled up in pain after the goddess Babd appears naked before them, and is finally killed. As is common in Ireland, there is an alternative version of how the men of Ulster became afflicted with the pangs, which tells of Cúchulainn going to live with the fairy Fedelm of the Long Hair, who after about a year appeared naked before the men, whereupon they were immediately stricken with the affliction.

There are many other early historical stories, mostly recorded by Roman writers, of Celtic women such as Boudica and other female warriors, who went

Sheela-na-gig with protruding tongue, Cloghan Castle.

into battle naked. In the mythological story "The Death of Finn," in the midst of a battle, Finn (styled elsewhere as Fionn Mac Cumhaill) sent a female messenger, Birgad, to offer terms to his opponents, but their response was to threaten to kill her if they ever saw her again. But Finn knew what he was doing, for Birgad lifted up her dress, "above the globe of her buttocks… her head, her tongue quivering," and they started to negotiate terms. A couple of sheela-na-gigs have fully protruding tongues, notably the figure on a quoin stone on Cloghan Castle in County Roscommon, as well as the legless figure found in the Figile River near Clonbullogue. Some, like the sheela-na-gig in Cavan Museum, have a small tongue-like object between their teeth, and of course, weathering may have obliterated such a feature on other figures.

It could be assumed from the above tales that the female genitals were a very powerful symbol of the goddess in her life-giving aspect, and as such, they would be a symbol that opposes war and forms of destruction. In other words, the vulva, as the source of life, was the natural opposite of death. However, this dualistic way of thinking is not really in keeping with the way the Celts usually embraced both sides of a meaning. Rather, it appears that the female genitals—or, less explicitly, female nakedness—were the source of both life and death, and as such, they were an even more powerful force than mere weap-

Sheela-na-gig on Bishop's Choral, Cashel.

ons. The goddess of death is also the goddess of life, as both life and death are mutually intertwined and share vital aspects. As the poet Nuala Ni Dhomhnaill has commented, "This image is so archaic and fundamental as to be all but forgotten in modern life. This is the as-yet-undifferentiated Mother of Life and Death. Her self-exhibition has nothing sexual or lascivious about it; rather, it is a reminder of something which, to us liberated moderns, is much more obscene and frightening.

The Bunratty Sheela-na-gig.

This is where you came from, and this is where you are going."

The many stories that centered around the actions of such a goddess are numerous and would have been widely and commonly transmitted as part of the rich oral storytelling of the Middle Ages. The Gaelic/Norman lords patronized such storytellers who were responsible for transmitting the history of the land, and it is certain that the image of the hag would have been even more vivid at the time when the sheela-na-gigs were being carved on their churches and castles.

Mythology tells us that Ireland has always been named after a female entity, either Banba, Fódla, or in its present incarnation as Éire: names of goddesses ruling over a land. And the land was originally inhabited by a large and diverse pantheon of tutelary goddesses who ruled over virtually every corner of the landscape.

Most of the deities who once existed in the land and minds of the people are now all but lost to us, but there are still numerous references to female entities, hags or wild witch-type wom-

Doon Castle.

Tullovin Castle.

en, in the lore and traditions of the countryside of Ireland, as well as hundreds of ancient monuments, dolmens, cairns, and standing stones that have female names or are related to the cailleach or hag. And nearly every castle has its tale of a witch or powerful female of some form, be it human or animal—often as a cat—attached to it. Glades, mountains, and the many mystical or menacing places in the natural world are almost always named after and inhabited by a female entity, while rivers and lakes, coursing their serpentine energy through the land, are entirely feminized in name and nature.

The world during the Middle Ages is a place in which the legends and stories still echoed among the people with an imperative that is barely comprehensible in our modern scientific era. It was a world in which the people would have been more familiar with the local stories of wise women, witches, hags, and the many female deities that inhabited the land, their attributes and behaviors still remembered, perhaps in great detail. And the people of this world were seeking to identify with the land and its traditions with a renewed intensity, brought about by the mixing of cultures—the Norman/English and the Gaels and Celts—and as a part of that quest for identity, a new tradition was formed: the craft of carving images of sacred female divinities in stone.

CHAPTER SIX

THE SYMBOLOGY OF THE SHEELA-NA-GIGS

ONE OF THE MORE CURIOUS ASPECTS of the sheela-na-gigs is that most of them appear rather crudely executed, as if created by unskilled hands. It is often suggested that they were the work of someone lacking the skill to create a more realistic image. Yet while many of them have crude appearances, there are also some in which the hand of more proficient masons is evident. The majority of the figures have, of course, undergone considerable weathering, but there are a few examples, such as the Ballylarkin figure, that clearly were created by skillful hands. Two figures from Ballinderry and Rahara, which have accompanying Celtic artwork, are carved with a skill comparable to any of the more commonly lauded Celtic carvings, such as High Crosses. This surely confirms that the carving of the sheela-na-gigs was at least as equally important as any of the other carvings that might adorn those buildings, if not more so.

The crudeness with which some figures appear to have been carved may in some instances be deliberate, the carvings left unfinished perhaps to accentuate their archaic otherworldliness. However, what is quite clear, and a fundamental aspect of the figures, is that they are carved in a tradition of symbolic rather than representational imagery, one that is deliberate and considered. Every sheela-na-gig is an individualistic representation of something: a myth-

Rahara Castle.

ological figure, an entity, or a divinity, rendered in symbolic form. This is one of the most intriguing and mysterious aspects of the subject, and it is also one of the major keys with which we can start to unlock an understanding of them.

In keeping with the tradition of Celtic art, sheela-na-gigs are arcane figures, and every aspect of the carvings—the stance, the display, the limbs and hands, the size and shape of their heads, the eyes and ears, the face or body grooves, the objects they hold, and the great variety of ways in which the central attribute, the genital organs, are featured—all of these odd, intriguing details have been deliberately chosen and held a definite symbolic meaning.

In the Celtic world, it was common to depict the gods and goddesses as non-human or even ugly in order to impress mortals with their power. Honor and reverence to a deity in Celtic art was visually demonstrated through use of plurality, exaggeration, or schematics, while energy, tension, asymmetry, and opposition also enhanced the potency of the designs. Unnecessary detail was abandoned in order to capture the numen—the divine essence—of an image, and as a result, these images were not hidebound by a rigid framework of realism. However bizarre and unnatural the deity appeared in earthly terms, this asymmetry in the features of an image functioned as a direct acknowledgment of power. This is not only true of the sheela-na-gigs but can be seen in almost all the Celtic images. For instance, the face carved on the stone head of the Beltany stone circle in County Donegal is very similar to many of the faces of the sheela-na-gigs, with its asymmetrical eyes, ears, and facial and neck striations.

The sheela-na-gigs from Errigal Keerogue Church and Tullaroan are good examples of this asymmetry. The first has one shoulder higher than the other, while the second has a stunted left leg. This might be less noticeable in many of the sheela-na-gigs, but often, a figure that appears superficially to be fairly balanced can be seen as asymmetric in features such as the ears or eyes.

The Beltany Head.

Many sheela-na-gigs have both one arm and one leg raised, a stance that is especially illustrated in the figure from Kiltinan Church. Such symbolism as the one-legged stance and the staring eyes are thought to be a concept that is of extreme antiquity. In her book The Metamorphosis of Baubo, Winifred Milius Lubell described this as "the stance of the magician." This is exactly how the hag is described in the myth of Da Derga's Hostel, in which she curses Conaire Mór when he refuses to allow her to spend the night in the hostel. There are many other instances in Irish literature where hags appear as one-eyed, one-handed, and one-footed, and are always occurring in magical and supernatural contexts.

In an unpublished paper, "Divine Deformity: the Plinian Races," Philip Bernhardt-House references several instances of mythological characters employing the magical stance. Cúchulainn, the great warrior-hero, who is also of divine ancestry, is said to have adopted a one-eyed, one-footed, and one-armed posture in order to carve a challenge in the letters of the Ogham script. In mythology, this is known as the corrguinecht posture (and was also used by the bards to accentuate a particularly powerful or scathing poem, in which context the pose was called the *glam dicenn*). After surviving many battles, the hero's death is finally brought about by a group of six magical women, who are said to have a single eye in their heads, a single arm, and a single leg.

The figure from Clonbulloge.

Central to the symbolism of the sheela-na-gigs is that powerful and evocative image, the vulva or yoni. This has been revered as the central and most powerful symbol for virtually all cultures since remote antiquity, and its use on cult objects or depictions of various goddesses in a state of display extends as far back as the Paleolithic era. In the sheela-na-gigs, it is frequently exaggerated in size, and its representation requires a frontal view, whether the figure was carved in relief or in the round.

The symbolism of the vulva is not meant to be erotic or obscene or intended to arouse sexual desire. Rather, it was initially thought to indicate not only human fertility but also the life force or an energy that emanated from the earth itself, in all its abundance, bounty, and creativity. This has led to the sheela-na-gigs being popularly regarded as fertility figures, but there is more to their symbology than just fertility.

Prehistoric goddess figures most often portray their fecundity by accentuating the main procreative features, such the belly and the breasts, often leaving out the sexual organs entirely. Many are portrayed seated, often accompanied by symbols of abundance and fertility, such as animals, food, or infants, and they usually have pronounced breasts. In contrast, only a few sheela-na-gigs look robust enough to be symbols of fertility. Almost all have very small breasts, if any at all, and look so lean that their ribs are showing. The only element that can be considered a symbol of fertility in the design of the sheela-na-gigs is the genitalia, but depiction of this part of the female anatomy alone does not represent fertility. When it is represented along with their other features, however, it becomes a much more potent image.

There is a great variety of ways in which the arms or hands of the sheela-na-gigs are used to indicate and draw attention to the vulva. The majority employ the significant gesture of both hands in front, directed toward the lower abdomen or vulva, but sometimes, the hands come from behind the buttocks or flexed thighs. This latter pose is a gesture of intensification, a means of accentuating the focus on this part of the anatomy. It is often varied with one hand passing in front of one thigh and the other hand passing from behind the other thigh, in a manner of intertwining and flowing, as displayed in the Ballinacarriga figure. A less common pose is where one hand is in front indicating the vulva and the other hand is resting on the thigh or knee. Some, like the serene Ballylarkin figure, merely point to it, and others, like the figure on Cloghan Castle, just grasp the legs.

The headless figure from Caherelly.

What is very intriguing is that parts of the vulva not directly involved in reproduction at all are often clearly portrayed. In some figures, the clitoris, the labia, and in several instances the anus are depicted, sometimes with an anatomical realism that contrasts sharply with the otherwise fantastical overall style.

The headless figure from Caherelly has a uniquely cavernous vulva and also a defined clitoris. Similar additional protrusions possibly depicting the clitoris are visible on a number of other figures. On some, this even includes the depiction of a hole beneath the vulva, which would logically represent the anus. Several of the figures have this clearly defined genital feature, including the figures from Ballyportry Castle and Glanworth Castle, but it is espe-

 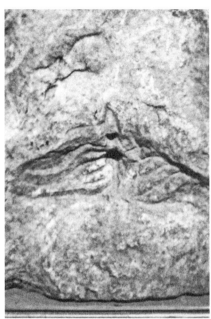

Left: Sheela-na-gig sold at auction in Dublin. Right: The abdominal area of the Ballyportry figure.

cially noticeable in the figure that was sold at auction in Dublin in 2003. Such anatomical precision is entirely unnecessary if the sole desire is to symbolize fecundity.

Burgusbeg.

Features such as these are entirely absent from all of the earlier goddess and fertility images, but some are very apparent on the Romanesque figures, many of which feature an anus. This probably has a very different context when it appears on the sheela-na-gigs, but it does suggest that certain themes might be running through the whole medieval period, whether or not the meaning remains the same.

Another peculiar feature found among the sheela-na-gigs is the unexplained objects descending from the vulva or lying underneath the legs of some figures. Something can be seen issuing from beneath the vulva of at least eight of the figures, and sometimes it appears almost like a secondary vulva or anus. At other times, it looks like more of a fluid. The sheela-na-gig over the doorway of Ballinderry Castle has a particularly evident flow of something from the vulva, which might represent her sacred essence or sexual potency in the form of menstrual blood or water. Another type of extra appendage below the vulva can be seen on several sheela-na-gigs, sometimes an oval-shaped depression, as on the figure on Cloghan Castle. On others, such as the Burgesbeg I figure, it is just a hole, and at Fantstown, it appears to be simply an extension of the vulva, though weathering may obscure its exact nature.

Fantastown.

The reason for this incongruous use of realism in the depiction of the genitalia may be to enhance the apotropaic function of the figures, but it may also go much deeper and could even be evidence of gnostic sexual practices in some of the more remote rural monastic communities. A recently discovered figure, revealed when the ivy was removed from the old church of Taughboy, has something that looks uncannily like male genitalia protruding below a defined vulva. It is also unique in being the only known sheela-na-gig to have been carved on a pyramid-shaped stone and erected on the very apex of the western wall. Binoculars or a telephoto lens are required to view this figure, so it is hardly an ideal position to place an image meant to warn against the sin of lust, yet just the kind of place one might position something that hints at a hidden practice within

Taughboy.

Behy.

the religious community. Curiously, Cloghan Castle is less than 1.5 kilometers away, and this also has a protrusion below the vulva. It is also one of only two sheela-na-gigs in the country with a fully protruding tongue.

Many references in both historic and folk-lore memory attest to a belief in the inherent power and ability of the female genitals to ward off evil forces. On the Isle of Man, women used to stride over the ceremonial bonfires, exposing their vulvae to the beneficial influence of the flame, and blessing it with their own power. The power of the female genitals to avert misfortune even includes the ability to calm a storm at sea through a woman exposing herself. Belief in its apotropaic potency continues today in many countries, such as India, where both the vulva and its symbolic image the sacred triangle are regarded as representations of divine power. In Christian art, the almond-shaped vesica pisces symbolizes the vulva, and is frequently depicted surrounding holy figures. Although its origin is seldom referred to, it was used by early Christians to represent the mystery of God's union with his mother-bride.

Rutland.

The dual representation of the vulva as both an abstract symbol and as a part of the natural female anatomy can be seen as the threshold through which all life emerges. Implicit in its symbolic use is the divine power that is associated with life, death, and rebirth, as well as the more occult notion in which the vulva or the vesica pisces symbolizes the point at which apparently separate forces or worlds simultaneously meet and divide.

A number of the sheela-na-gigs are depicted with one arm raised, either pointing to the head or else straight up. The figures from Behy, Tullovin, and Burgesbeg II have their arm raised to the ear, as if to signify attention or concentrated listening, and such an emphasis on the impression of watchfulness is an attitude which would suit well a figure that acts in a guardian role or has an apotropaic function.

The majority of the rest of this type have their hand located somewhere near the side of their face, as can be seen on the figures from Tinakill and Clomantagh, while the

Kiltinane Castle.

figures from Aghadoe and Rutland are pointing upward with unidentified objects in their left hands. The only example in the whole of the British Isles and Ireland of a sheela-na-gig shown with both arms raised is the figure on Kiltinan Castle figure, and she is shown with a round object in her left hand.

Similar to the type with one arm raised is the sheela-na-gig with one leg raised. This is best exemplified in the figures from Swords, Ballaghmore, and Kiltinan Church, who look as if they are doing a jig. A number of other sheela-na-gigs such as those at Cooliagh More, Shanrahan, Blackhall, and Tara have to a lesser extent their leg slightly raised, perhaps to simply create an asymmetrical feature. The Shanrahan figure has one foot turned inward, and the Sheela at Doon Castle is depicted facing outward but has both feet pointing to her right. The only other examples of this are the sheela-na-gig from Ringaskiddy, which has both feet turned inward, while the sheela-na-gigs from Swords and Tullaroan each have one leg that is considerably shorter than the other.

It is perhaps not surprising that the heads are most often one of the most striking features of the sheela-na-gigs, for, in keeping with the depiction of divine images in Celtic art, the head is often abnormally large in relation to the torso. In a number of figures, the head

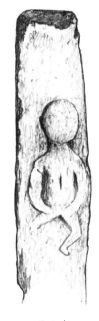

Swords.

Lustymore.

is distinctly triangular, and this is even accentuated by a pointed chin. The figure from Lustymore Island is perhaps the best example of this style and is particularly relevant, since it now stands alongside the possibly older and classically Celtic Janus figure, with its triangular head and pointed chin.

The prominent, clearly demarcated, otherworldly eyes of many sheela-na-gigs are frequently depicted as crooked-looking or asymmetrical. The sheela-na-gig from Ballinacarriga Castle has a benign countenance that is greatly accentuated by the way the left eye appears closed while the right eye is wide open and is surrounded by a crescent around it, perhaps symbolizing her supernatural status. The closed eye, the left eye in particular, is seen as a way of gaining otherwise hidden knowledge, mostly connected to the supernatural. A blind or closed left eye is obviously linked to the supernatural and associated with having access to otherwise hidden knowledge.

Ears may be absent, but when they are present, there is a large variation in the way they are depicted. Often, they accentuate the asymmetrical nature of the figure, as at Ballinacarriga and Ballinderry, while the right ear of the figure in Fethard Abbey is extremely large but the left ear is smaller. The sheela-na-gig on Redwood Castle is more unusual, for what is probably a crescent-shaped ear floats by the right side of her face and she has no ear at all on the other

Head of the Ballinacarriga
Sheela-na-gig.

side. Although this figure is a long way up on the castle wall, this ear is quite prominent, as if the carver wanted to attach some special importance to it. The most recent sheela-na-gig to be discovered, the figure from Clootymurraghy in east Galway, seems to have been deliberately carved with her face inclined to her right, which allowed the depiction of the large left ear.

A few figures, especially those at Kil-

One of the Sheela-na-gigs
from Scregg Castle

Fethard Abbey.

sarkan and one of the figures from Scregg, have prominent cow-like ears. The cow was highly regarded by the Celts and held a particularly prominent status in the Gaelic world, whose ancestral mother of the gods was Bóande, the white cow goddess, after whom the Brú na Bóinne is named. The occurrence of cow-like ears on certain Irish figures suggests that they represent a particular aspect of divinity.

Tongues are evident on many of the Romanesque images; indeed, it is one of the more common features of many different types of figures carved by those earlier religious artists. It is perhaps surprising, then, that if the sheela-na-gig image is derived from an earlier Romanesque prototype, only two sheela-na-gigs, the figures from Cloghan Castle and Clonbulloge, have a fully protruding tongue in the way that it is often depicted in Romanesque art. Small, tongue-like features can be seen on some figures like the sheela-na-gigs,

Head of the Cloghan figure.

The Chloran Sheela-na-gig.

usually those with pronounced teeth, such as the figures from Cavan and Killua, and on some stone heads, as the Beltany stone head from County Donegal. Meanwhile, on the double-sided Janus figure from Boa Island, the tongue is protruding on one face, but not on the other.

More common amongst the sheela-na-gigs is the showing of teeth, which appears to suggest a more fearsome but probably equally apotropaic message as the protruding tongue. A grim row of incised and fairly frightening-looking teeth appears on numerous sheela-na-gigs from Cavan, Chloran, Bunratty, Fethard, Moate, Lavey, and Clonmel. Teeth are more ambiguously represented on the figures at Rahan, where beading around the upper lip may represent teeth, and at Glanworth Castle, where short vertical lines are probably indicative of teeth.

The heads of many sheela-na-gigs are conspicuously bald, but some have a rim of hair or a type of a headdress, which is sometimes very simply rep-

Hollymount.

resented as a short frame around the face, such as on the Rahan figure. This is also seen on a number of the English figures, such as those at Ampney St. Peters, Tugford, and Romsey. The lines across the forehead of the Cavan sheela-na-gig could possibly be a special headdress. On the Kilsarkan and Tullovin sheela-na-gigs, the rim of the headdress is indicated in more elaborate detail, while the figure from Castle Widenham has a very strange box-like headdress with snippets down both sides of the head, one of which reaches the right shoulder.

A recently discovered figure at Hollymount in County Mayo has a particularly pronounced hat, to which comparisons have been drawn to the hats that some women wore in medieval art. But it differs quite a lot from the conical hats most commonly depicted, so it is also feasible that it is a Coptic-style headpiece of some kind.

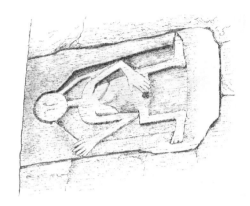

Clomantagh.

The sheela-na-gigs from Ballinderry and Rahara are sometimes described as having plaits down either side of their heads, but what is described as hair is actually a pleated ornament of interlacing knotwork. At Clomantagh Castle, the figure was mistakenly described by Andersen as having "an absurd form of flying plaits," but she is actually set in a recessed frame that follows closely around her body. On her left-hand side is a raised slender band that seems to protrude from the side of her head, and runs down to her arm. What this singular slender band represents is a mystery, but it seems unlikely that it is any form of hair or plaits. The recently discovered figure at Clootymurraghy also has something like a plait around her in the form of a twisted rope pattern.

Apart from the cavities representing the genitals, holes also appear in odd positions on a number of figures. By far

The most holed Sheela-na-gig from the church of Seir Kieran.

The 'four-eyed' Taghmon figure.

the most spectacular example of this is the figure from Seir Kieran. This figure has so many and such pronounced holes right across its body that it can be difficult to be certain what exactly represents the vulva. It also has holes in the top of its head and beneath the figure. Yet the largest hole is just below the normal location of the pudenda and goes up into the body, which suggests the drilling was done from below. Despite speculation to the contrary, it is likely that these holes are an original feature of the sculpture before it was erected on the wall of the church. There are also holes in the heads of several other figures; the holes in the head of the two-faced Boa Island Janus figure show that they were not confined to the sheela-na-gigs. It has been suggested that these figures show a persistence of traditions associated with the Celtic horned god Cernunnos.

Another very strange, freestanding figure from Knockharley also has a small, neat hole drilled through the top of her head and another below her vulva, and the figure from Swords has what looks like a tiny hole just above her vulva on her abdomen. The Abbeylara figure also has three holes around the area of her breast, and the strange Taghmon figure has four eyes or four holes across her forehead.

Perhaps the most universal feature seen on the sheela-na-gigs is lines across the chest area that are generally regarded as ribs. It is curious that the carvers should choose to depict ribs, and it may be that it is mere convention or may have a more arcane meaning. Two fairly recently identified sheela-na-gigs, Rutland and Tullaroan, have distinct ribbing that extends across the whole chest area, and some figures have ribbing on various parts of the body, including the arms and the legs, making it difficult to determine what, if anything, represents the breasts. On many of the figures, the ribbing has been worn away and is only noticeable on close inspection, but even if faint, this is present on many of the sheela-na-gigs. Various explanations for the significance of these body grooves or rib-bing have been given by research-ers, and it is generally thought that they signify emancipation, death, or suffering. Behind this interpretation is the desire to denigrate the shee-la-na-gigs by suggesting that they are anti-sexual and, as some have suggested, represent "cadaverous specimens," or even worse, "women in the later stages of syphilis."

Clonmel.

This cadaverous look, however, parallels the description of the hag in the mythologies, and it has been suggested that it is an illustration of a death-in-life attitude, where the upper part of the figure may mirror mor-tality and the lower half (with the vulva) the source of further life. That these lines depict ribs seems a very strong argument, if it was not for the fact that there are the previously mentioned examples where they extend beyond the rib area, as well as examples where numerous other lines are also found on the breasts and other parts of the body, apart from the chest area. An example of this is the Clonmel figure, which has ribbing also extending from the breasts to the armpits.

Another type of body grooving is a band-like feature across the abdomen that occurs on the sheela-na-gigs from both Moate and Tracton Abbey, as well as on the Janus figure from Boa Island, interestingly. The sheela-na-gig from Clonlara was also once noted as having remarkably clear tool marks across the stomach, but this feature is hardly visible now, due to weathering. The Boa Island figure has striations across its arms, and the well-preserved figure at Aghadoe not only has accentuated ribs but also clearly defined linear strokes across her arms and legs.

Noticeable on a number of sheela-na-gigs is the clear presence of stria-tions or lines that are carved across their foreheads, cheeks, and sides of the head and neck. For instance, the sheela-na-gigs from Ballinderry, Moate, and Cavan have strong lines across the forehead, and on the Kiltinan Castle figure,

The Janus Figure.

the lines are carried across her forehead to the sides of her head. It has been suggested that these lines represent wrinkles or an intensification of an expression, such as age, which would be in line with many of the mythological descriptions of the hag.

On at least three sheela-na-gigs, the striation marks occur across the cheek in more of the manner of a scar or a tattoo than as a sign of character. The Fethard Abbey figure has a streaked cheek, and the fearsome-looking sheela-na-gig nearby on the old town wall has a striated chevron-like pattern on her left cheek, which begins at the base and is virtually identical to the patterned heads of the Janus figure from Boa Island. On the Athlone sheela-na-gig, there is a striated pattern of three marked lines incised across the left cheek and less distinct traces on the other cheek. Clearly incised striation marks can be seen on the figures from Killinaboy, beginning from the base of the neck and going up toward the bottom of the chin, and the sheela-na-gig from Seir Kieran also bears slight traces of striated cheeks and more definite streaks on the neck. On the figure from Clonoulty, there are clear indications of striations on the neck and possibly along the side of her head, although unfortunately it has been rather badly damaged.

These facial lines might represent a form of tattooing, which is, of course, a very ancient custom common to indigenous people throughout the world and still serves as a form of self-identification today. In tribal societies, it was primarily associated with some coming-of-age ritual, such as puberty rites, and although body and face painting were used in many ceremonies, actual tattooing which involved physically scarring the body held a much more powerful and obviously permanent symbolic importance. The lines could then indicate the mark of a wise woman or healer.

In view of the fact that the current accepted Irish rendering of Sheela-na-Gig is *sile ne g'coch*, a name which is generally regarded as meaning "sheela of the paps or breasts," one might expect that these might feature prominently on the figures. Yet more often than not, the opposite is the case. In most of the sheela-na-gigs, the breasts are only slightly indicated. However, in some instances, such as the figure from Caherelly Castle, they are of normal size, although they are never exaggerated.

Aghadoe.

Several sheela-na-gigs are depicted with more than one pair of breasts, and these are often described as representing a sagging bosom. This is most noticeable on the figure from Ballylarkin, where the lower breasts could be regarded as sagging. On the sheela-na-gig at Aghadoe, there are two sets of breasts that are of the same size as well as distinct ribbing, so they do not seem to represent a sagging of the chest. This figure has also the distinction of having some very odd nodules low down on the arms, and is holding a strange notched object with the left arm. This is the only figure so far discovered with such features.

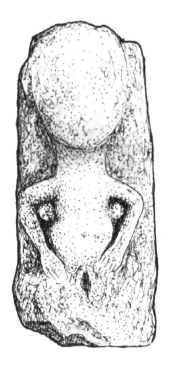

Birr.

Lavey

On some figures, the breasts are even located directly under the armpits, such as on the sheela-na-gig from Birr, where the breasts are shaped like round balls. This can be very clearly seen on the sheela-na-gigs from Ballinderry, Rahara, and Ballyporty Castle. Even more peculiar is the Burgesbeg sheela-na-gig, who has two large round circles on her lower stomach.

The Lavey Church sheela-na-gig holds a circular disk that is tucked under her left arm, yet confusingly, the outline of the circle is also incised on top of her arm. A round circle, which is possibly a bellybutton but appears too high to be so, appears midway between the chest and stomach on a quite a few figures.

The Kiltinan Church sheela-na-gig was unusual for having two nipples on her left breast and only one on her right, the additional symbolism of triplicity accentuating her overall magical representation. At Ballinacarriga, the figure also appears to be represented with an odd number of nipples, as there appears to be only one on her left breast and none on her right breast.

This strong association with the circular form, whether it be in the guise of a circular object or round hole or simply engraved on some part of the figure's body, is perhaps the most surprising and prevalent aspect of the sheela-na-gig symbolism. The figure from Aghadoe Castle is no exception, as the most unique features of this carving are the strange, round nodules very clearly carved into the wrists, three on her downward-pointing right arm and at least two but possibly originally three on her upraised left arm. The Ballinderry Castle figure is also connected with the circular motif, as three geometric circles surround her as part of the design around her on the keystone.

The sheela-na-gig from Behy Castle in County Sligo is very unusual in that

Liathmore

it is painted red. This might have been done fairly recently, but according to the owners of the farm on which it is situated, it has been for as long as anyone can remember, and indeed the paint is very old-looking. The figure was removed from the nearby castle at least a century ago and was placed in a protective position, so it is one of the best-preserved figures. Traces of red coloring have been noted on other figures from both Ireland and Britain, and a figure from Wales is said to have traces of paint "the color of blood." Red was the color most frequently associated with the otherworld or the supernatural, and to be stained red meant to be chosen by the goddess as a king. In the Irish language, *ruadh*, meaning "red," can also mean "royal," while in Irish mythology, the hag was also associated with this color. In the story of Macha and the sons of Dithorba, she changed into the form of a leper, having rubbed rye dough and red from a bog all over herself.

There is also the question of why some figures are set reclining horizontally into a quoin stone on the corner of a building. This is mostly seen among the castles' sheela-na-gigs, but is also known from churches such as Liathmore, Kiltinan, and the Rock of Cashel. It is quite possible, of course, that some figures originally set in a standing position may have been reerected on their side, but why they should have done this is unknown. The word *quoin* refers to a keystone and generally means a stone set in such a way as to strengthen the structure. Most of the sheela-na-gigs are not carved onto stones that are essential to the construction of the building, as was shown by the blatant removal of the figure that was formerly a quoin stone on Kiltinan Church.

One figure that was definitely created to fit onto the corner of a building is the unique and legless sheela-na-gig that had been tossed into the river near Clonbulloge, but most of the figures set sideways can be seen to have been deliberately carved onto blocks that were to be used as quoin stones. It is not known when the tradition of setting the figures sideways began, but the sheela-na-gig at Liathmore, which is thought to be one of the earliest, has downward-pointing pellets carved alongside the figure. The figure is carved in one piece, which suggests that the reclining position was part of the carver's intent.

The practice of setting figures sideways has also been described in Chapter 3, in relation to two figures from the earlier phase of Killinaboy Church that were inserted horizontally into the wall of the later-rebuilt church. Both of these figures are carved in a way that shows they would have originally formed cornerstones, but why they have been placed on their sides is a mystery and is probably not unconnected with the reason we find some sheela-na-gigs on their side. Two of the strange figures found in the ruins of the old church on White Island in Lough Erne were also found inserted sideways into the wall. These were carved earlier than most of the sheela-na-gigs, though one appears as if it could be related to the genre.

What comes through most clearly is that the various poses or postures appear to establish a supernatural context for the display of the figures. These postures and the symbolism of the figures can be seen as laying the background against which representation of divine power, the exhibiting of the genitalia, takes place. Other important features, such as the face and body tattooing and the holding of circular objects, all imply a divine status for the images.

Such features may well have been inspired by the then-renowned and vivid descriptions of the hag in mythology: the divine feminine who was responsible for the fortunes, fertility, and prosperity of her territory and whose primary purpose may have been one of warding off evil and misfortune. She was the personification of the most revered and yet feared aspects of the world, a symbol of life and fertility as well as portraying death. Viewed in the light of the symbolic tradition of Celtic art, the figures come to represent a ritual, a divine rite, frozen in symbolic enactment around the central, all-powerful image of life and death.

CHAPTER SEVEN

EARLY PROTOTYPES AND RELATED FIGURES

ONE OF THE MAIN FACTORS that allows credence to the proposition that the sheela-na-gigs arose as part of Romanesque iconography is the question of whether there are any figures in Ireland that predate the figures found on those eleventh- and twelfth-century churches. Any figures that could have been carved before this era would necessitate a complete re-appraisal of the origin of the figures, perhaps even opening up the possibility of an opposing scenario whereby the Irish sheela-na-gig may have influenced the creation of the Romanesque exhibitionist figures.

Those most likely to be established as very early figures are the few examples that are found on pillar stones. While the majority of sheela-na-gigs are nearly always carved onto slabs, which could be incorporated into the masonry of a building, a figure on a pillar stone is of special significance.

One of the most important examples, and certainly the most controversial, is the rather indistinct figure carved in relief onto a standing stone in the churchyard at Tara. The figure is very worn, curiously weathered despite it facing away from the prevailing wind and rain, which suggests that it may be of great age. There is some dispute about the figure, but recent Lidar 3-D scanning of the figure shows that it can be nothing other than a sheela-na-gig. It is carved in relief on the stone, and the tooling can be seen on the area around

Left: Blocc and Bluigne, ceremonial entrance to Tara.
Right: The Sheela-na-gig on Adamnan's Pillar.

the figure, suggesting that it was a later addition to an already ancient stone. The fact that it stands on the most important sacred ceremonial site of Ireland, the place where the ancient kings of Ireland ritually entered into sacral marriage with the goddess of the land, makes this a central figure.

The stone known as St. Adamnan's Pillar is one of a pair of stones called Blocc and Bluigne. They are quite unlike anything created in the medieval era and are said to have played an integral role in the sovereignty or coronation ceremonies that were carried out at Tara. It has been suggested that St. Adamnan's Pillar was originally a caryatid, a pillar stone that was used as a support in an earlier church, possibly as a doorjamb. It has even been suggested that both of these stones may have originally flanked the entrance of a thirteenth-century church that was demolished in 1823, leaving almost no trace, and then replaced by the present church.

The Blocc and Bluigne stones lay near the perimeter of one of the more important prehistoric earthworks at Tara, an enclosure known as the Rath of the Synods, which, as its name implies, is connected to the early foundation of Christianity in Ireland. Nearby is the Teach Midchúarta or the House

Stepaside.

The gate post at Drynam
House, Swords.

of the Women, which in pre-Christian times could well have been the foundation or college of women residing at the site. The sheela-na-gig here may illustrate how the use of this image was reserved as a special symbol at places especially dedicated to women. A sheela-na-gig here on St. Adamnan's Pillar has obvious implications, while not knowing the date of origin of the stone and its evocative figure leaves them standing uncertainly between the Christian church and the ancient earthworks of a former era.

Saint Adamnan, born in 624 A.D., is one of the most central of the post-Patrician saints, being the biographer of Columba, the founder of the Celtic monastic community on Iona in the western Isles of Scotland, and later a bishop of that foundation. Most pertinent to his memory at Tara is his "Law of Adomnán," which gave immunity to women and children during warfare. There is also a very worn figure over a window of the old nunnery on Iona that is said to be a sheela-na-gig and another next to the entrance door on Kilvickeon

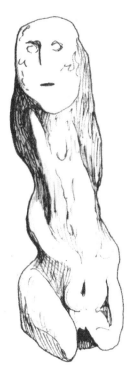

Knockarley.

Church, a short distance away on the Island of Mull. Though both of these figures are very worn and it is not possible to positively identify them as sheela-na-gigs, they do both exhibit certain features that strongly suggest they could be, while their location and positions on those buildings also aligns them with the way sheela-na-gigs are traditionally located in Ireland. The west of Scotland was at that time known as Dál Riata or Dalriadagh and was virtually a part of Ireland, being ruled and inhabited by Irish clans whose memory is retained through the use of the Scottish Gaelic language, a derivative of Middle Irish.

Another sheela-na-gig that was possibly also carved onto a pillar stone was being used as a gate post for Drynam House near Swords, and it is also carved in relief onto a pillar stone. Her right leg is raised, as if doing a jig. Like at the figure at Tara, this figure may have originally been built into the doorway of a medieval building, possibly a church built during the early Christian period in the vicinity. These earlier churches were often constructed from huge stone blocks that flanked their doorways, a feature that is rarely seen on the churches built during the later Middle Ages.

Another significant figure can be found carved in relief on a cross-shaped stone erected beside an ancient holy well near an early monastic site at Stepaside, in southern County Dublin. This stone is quite unique in that it has on its reverse side a carving of a circle and other possible symbolism that is too worn to decipher. This is a very different figure from most of the sheela-na-gigs, and there is disagreement about in exactly which genre it should be placed. Yet it displays a unique style of carving that cannot be related to any of the known images of the period, and having hands placed where the genitals would be, it suggests a close affinity with the sheela-na-gigs. Edith Guest considered this figure to be of an early origin, as it is carved on a cross of a type that would usually be ascribed to the early Christian period, possibly seventh to ninth centu-

Sheela-na-gig re-erected on wall by St. Patrick's Well in the old monastic village of Aghagower, County Mayo.

An unusual sheela-na-gig with legs tucked up and hands grasping the knees was formerly set up over a gateway at the convent of St. Peter's Port but thought to be from an earlier monastery. Now in Athlone Castle Museum, County Westmeath.

An impish-looking sheela-na-gig can be seen on a quoin stone on Ballaghmore Castle, County Laoise.

The sheela-na-gig on Ballinacarriga Castle, County Cork is set high on the east wall just below the level that was used as a church.

Detail of the sheela-na-gig on Ballinacarriga Castle.

The sheela-na-gig at Ballyfinboy in County Tipperary is on an early dry-stone castle that is fast crumbling away.

Sheela-na-gig from Ballyportry Castle, County Clare with extraordinarily detailed sexual organs. Now in the Clare Museum, Ennis.

The small sheela-na-gig carved into the window lintel on the church at Ballyvourney, County Cork is still regularly rubbed by the many pilgrims to this ancient shrine.

This unique legless sheela-na-gig with protruding tongue was found having been thrown into the Figile River near Clonbullogue, County Offaly.

Left: One of the best-preserved sheela-na-gigs was originally on the now-fallen Behy Castle in County Sligo, having been kept for many years in a sheltered position. No one knows when or why it was painted red. Right: Now in the National Museum, Dublin the sheela-na-gig from Birr, County Offaly was probably used as a corbel in an early church no longer in existence.

A well-preserved sheela-na-gig from the 13th-century Blackhall Castle, in County Kildare and now in private possession.

Thousands of visitors to the famous Rock of Cashel pass close by this sheela-na-gig yet few notice her set horizontally on a quoin stone on the 'Bishops Palace.'

Late sheela-like figure on the bridge over the 18th-century canal at Clonlara, County Limerick.

A rare early acrobatic sheela on the doorway of the Nun's Chapel
at Clonmacnoise, County Offaly.

The sheela-na-gig on Doon Castle in County Offaly is set horizontally on a quoin stone and has tiny breasts at the centre of the chest.

This well-preserved sheela-na-gig was only recently recognised in a farmyard in east County Galway. As well as being a rare example of a figure set within a decorative border, there is also an indentation representing a protruding tongue. Provenance unknown and now privately owned. Photo courtesy of Gary Dempsey, Lidar Project, UCG.

Now in Cavan County Museum, Ballyjamesduff, this startling figure
was probably deliberately damaged.

This strange figure in the old Abbey in the village of Fethard in County Tipperary is generally thought to be a sheela-na-gig despite that the abdominal portion is badly damaged.

The rather startling sheela-na-gig on the old town wall at Fethard in County Tipperary, adjacent to the main gateway and overlooking the nearby river. Known locally as 'the Witch on the Wall.'

One of the largest sheela-na-gigs in the country is set within a well-defined frame prominently facing the main courtyard/entrance to Dunnaman Castle in County Limerick.

Position of the
Sheela-na-gig

The sheela-na-gig on a quoin stone on Fantastown Castle in County Limerick is set into the eastern wall and is difficult to see at most times of the day.

Sheela-na-gig above the doorway of Killinaboy church, formerly known as an image of St. Inghean Bhuidhe, the founding saint of the church. Corofin, County Clare.

Color Section

Left: Recent photograph of the sheela-na-gig at Killinaboy church.
Right: Figure photographed in the 1970s.

This cherubic sheela-like figure was carved on the underside of
Bishop Arthur Wellesley's crypt. It is now stored in St. Brigit's Church
in Kildare town, County Kildare.

The strange armless figure above a window on Kilsarkan church in County Kerry
has been well rubbed in the area of the genitalia

SHEELA-NA-GIG: Sacred Celtic Images of Feminine Divinity

Now housed in Cavan County Museum, Ballyjamesduff. This stern sheela-na-gig with a
curious circular object on the left arm was originally on Lavey church east of Cavan town.

Decorated panel from an earlier church with upside-down sheela-na-gig inserted into later reconstructed church at Rathblathmaic, Countu Clare

Close up of the Rathblathmaic sheela-na-gig.

The early cross-shaped pillar set up by a spring near the old monastic site of Stepaside in south County Dublin has a curious sculpted sheela-na-gig carved on one side and a circle with vague traces of another similar figure on the other side.

Two stones set on the perimeter of the main enclosures on the Hill of Tara feature prominently in the mythology of this famous site. The sheela-na-gig on the taller pillar stone is only faintly visible, suggesting that it is of great age.

IRISH SHELAH—NA—GIG.
FOUND AT
CHLORAN CO:WESTMEATH.
(Witt Coll:258)

From County Westmeath, the figure originating from Chloran church
that was removed to the British Museum, London in the 19th century.

ry. But even if it proves to be of a later origin, it is still almost certainly a figure, which throws some doubt on the theory of a Romanesque origin. Recent 3-D imaging has revealed a second figure lurking ethereally behind the circle on the back of the stone.

The curious figure from Knockharley is another extraordinarily unique carving and is difficult to classify, though clear indications of a vulva show that it is part of the sheela-na-gig tradition. It is a freestanding sculpture carved of local sandstone, and it appears as if the stone was specifically chosen, such that it required only minor modifications. The most distinctive feature is its elongated neck topped by a face that is inclined toward the right. The right hand lies across the belly, and the left hand is laid on the thigh, while the vulva is clearly marked with a small incision surrounded by a very thick raised oval rim. Local historian John Feehan considered that this figure might be of an early Christian date, but the fact that it is a unique freestanding sculpture, which would have been nearly impossible to erect on a building, makes it particularly difficult to place into a datable context.

Two important ancient figures can currently be found in the grounds of the old Caldragh Church on Boa Island, at the northern end of Lower Lough Erne in County Fermanagh. One of these is the aforementioned double-faced Janus figure that is thought to have originated from an ancient site on the island. It is currently dated to around the ninth century but may be much older. The arms are crossed over, and the lower half of the figure has gone missing, but there is no mistaking the characteristic Celtic expression. A chevron-like pattern of tattoos extending from the side of its head to the cheeks is virtually identical to the markings on the fearsome-looking sheela-na-gig on the old town wall at Fethard. Several other features, such as a large head, the tongue poking out, a waistband, and striation marks extending across the arms, are reminiscent of other markings found on numerous sheela-na-gigs.

Placed near the Janus figure is a large freestanding sculpture that is obviously a sheela-na-gig, which originates from an early monastery on nearby Lustymore Island. The legs of the figure are very hard to make out, but the hands are gesturing toward the vulva, although the figure is so worn that the actual vulva is not now clearly indicated. The style of this figure, with its large head and pointed chin, suggests that it is of similar tradition as the Janus figure, if not carved by the same hand, while other features such as the broad-

White Island.

lipped mouth are shared not only by the Janus figure but also the sheela-na-gig from Cavan.

These figures from Tara, Swords, Stepaside, Knockharley, and Lustymore all illustrate the possibility that the sheela-na-gig motif was known before the twelfth century. Of these figures, two are on pillar stones, one is on a cross slab, and the others are freestanding sculptures, suggesting that they may have originated in the wooden churches that predated the stone churches. Each of them is clearly carved in the sheela-na-gig tradition, and they appear to be the earliest native Irish examples of sheela-na-gigs, though it would appear that it was a rare motif that was used sparingly and was probably regarded as having a particular potency.

On White Island, on Lough Erne, are six extraordinary figures dated to between the ninth and eleventh centuries that were found on the site of an old church. One of these, a cross-legged figure with the hands and arms resting across the thighs, was originally believed to be a sheela-na-gig, but it is quite different and there is no clear indication of a vulva, so it is not now classed in that genre. The large head is typical, but the broad, grinning mouth with its upturned corners is a unique feature. It has the eyes of a sheela-na-gig, one round and the other diamond-shaped, giving it that typical magical look. This figure is also unusual in that she is wearing a short cloak-like mantle, which the antiquarian George Victor Du Noyer supposed represented a rheno, or secular dress, which suggests it represents a clergywoman. The figure was broken on the top after one workman employed to clean up the church site took such a dislike to it that he took a swipe at it with his spade.

Two of the figures from White Island were rebuilt horizontally into the south wall of the twelfth- and thirteenth-century church, one beside a late Roman-

Left: The Bishop's Stone, Killadeas.

Carndonagh.

esque-style doorway and the other in the eastern gable. This church appears to have been built on the site of an earlier monastic foundation, and there are historical records of monasteries consisting entirely of wooden churches that existed during this period in this part of Lough Erne. One of these was called Devenish Bavagh and another Eoinis, and it is possible the White Island figures originated from one of these early monasteries. These stone figures on Boa Island and White Island all precede the medieval sheela-na-gigs and must be taken into account in the search for prototypes that show the descent of related styles and motifs, from early Christian to medieval settings.

In Killadeas Graveyard, also in County Fermanagh, is another unusual stone known as the Bishop's Stone that is similar in style to the White Island

Figure on High Cross, Clonmacnoise.

figures and is believed to date to the seventh or eighth century. On the west side of the stone is what looks like a pagan idol carved in deep relief with an interlaced pattern, and on the south side is a bishop or abbot carved in low relief, shown in profile walking westward, holding a bell and crozier. The figure has been compared to the sheela-na-gigs, for beside the large head and abbreviated body, it has a vertically sloping scar or tattoo on its left cheek similar to that of the Kiltinan Church figure.

Further north at Carndonagh, on the Inishowen peninsula in Donegal, are two so-called guardian stones that stand alongside one of the earliest high crosses in Ireland, dated to the seventh century. The guardian stones are thought to be from a century or two later and are said to originate from the nearby monastic site, established in 442 A.D. These stones are carved with a mixture of symbols, but on one side is a figure carved in low relief, the main features of which are very prominent circular designs, like round ears placed on the top of the head and the hands held across the stomach. There is also a clearly outlined round ball or disc below the right elbow and an indentation where the genitals would be. It has been suggested that it may be a sheela-na-gig, but the figure is now so badly weathered that this interpretation must be considered dubious. It is, however, a very early carving and probably played its role as a prototype for the medieval sheela-na-gigs, especially considering the evidence for its guardian role.

The association of sheela-na-gigs and high crosses can be seen in the figure on the tenth-century northern cross at Clonmacnoise, which was classed by Edith Guest as a sheela-na-gig. The figure can be found on the south side of the cross and has entwining legs that have best been called Cernunnos-like. The figure is of a similar motif to the sheela-na-gigs, and its inclusion as part of the decoration of this high cross signifies its importance as an earlier predecessor. Similar sheela-like figures also appear on Muiredach's High Cross at Monasterboice, which is dated to 924 A.D., and the eleventh-century high cross at Drumcliff in County Sligo, on which are two standing figures with one hand each indicating toward their lower abdomens. Clearly, there are instances in which a sheela-like motif was used in relation to certain stone figures carved either singularly, or as part of a greater ornamental composition on high crosses, prior to the Romanesque and during the early Christian period.

Cernunnos, God of Plenty.

Professor Etienne Rynne suggested that the forerunners of the sheela-na-gig motif, for both the Romanesque and medieval Irish figures, were associated with a fertility cult that merged with Cernunnos, the Celtic god of plenty, who is depicted on the second-century B.C. Gundestrup cauldron. Rynne believed that this association with Cernunnos, who is also shown in a squatting or cross-legged posture, would account for the medieval protection aspect and that the unique combination of this posture and the display of the vulva have antecedents in pagan Celtic times.

Several fascinating examples have been brought to light that appear to show a pagan Celtic background for the sheela-na-gigs. One of the earliest examples occurs on the terminals of a fine gold armlet, where the hands of a small figure are grasping or touching what appears to be her vulva, much in the manner of many sheela-na-gigs. She also has an owl-like bird perched on her head and fittingly invokes Rynne's concept of a mistress of the wild beasts,

The bone pin from Annagh Castle.

counterpart to Cernunnos, who is also known as the god of the wild beasts and associated with fertility.

The amulet was discovered in a late fifth- or fourth-century B.C. grave in Reinheim, Germany. Another early figure from a stele in Hofheim, Germany, could actually be mistaken for a sheela-na-gig, with her exaggerated head and squat, reduced body, except that she is said to date from between 83 and 121 A.D. An additional early example dating to the second century A.D. is a stone carving portraying a seated mother goddess that was found deep in a well at Caerwent in Wales. The carving is typically Celtic in appearance with indications of tattoos between her breasts.

In Ireland, pagan beliefs and practices continued well into Christian times, and it was suggested by Rynne that "it is possible to find in an Irish context the presence of apparent descendants of the pagan Celtic cult figures." An example he gives of this is a little figure grasping its tightly updrawn and bent legs, which is delicately carved on the head of a bone pin found near Newbridge, County Kildare, and believed to date from the latter eighth or ninth century. Another bone pin was actually included in the original 1894 list of sheela-na-gigs and was described as "an ancient ivory carving of the class popularly called sheela-na-gigs, measuring 1.5 inches high and forming apparently the top of a pin, found close to Annagh Castle on the edge of Lough Derg, County Tipperary."

Often, the only other form of decoration found in conjunction with the sheela-na-gigs is the closely allied motif of the stone head. Stone heads functioned as a symbol of the divine, a source of prosperity and fertility, and were often regarded as an apotropaic instrument to ward off evil from the individual and from the community as a whole. Like the sheela-na-gigs, they were also regarded in local tradition to be representations of ecclesiastic or royal personages. Features such as tattooing of the face or neck are often strikingly similar to the sheela-na-gigs, suggesting a certain overlap of traditions. The cult of the human head was an integral part of pagan Irish religion and ceremony during the Celtic Iron Age, and this is corroborated not only by numerous examples of pre-Christian human heads in stone but by the evidence of early literature, where the merits of heroes are judged by the number of severed enemy heads they possess.

The importance of the head, either singularly or in an exaggerated form, such as in Celtic idol sculpture, did not disappear with the coming of Christianity. On the contrary, there seemed to be an even greater proliferation of the motif on churches, abbeys, and castles built during the medieval period, a resurgence of its use that is contemporaneous with the rise of the sheela-na-gigs. There is no doubt that heads appear in great number during the Romanesque era in Ireland, the Romanesque doorway at Clonfert Abbey being a classic example. Through the comparison of the sheela-na-gigs with stone heads, it is arguable that such similarities go beyond mere physical likeness, and this supports the suggestion that the background for the emergence of the sheela-na-gigs can be found in the same pagan past.

Wooden carvings are often referred to in relation to sheela-na-gigs, and it has been suggested that the stone figures perpetuate images of wood that existed during an earlier period. Some very interesting wooden images have come to light, and indeed some have all the appearances of being the direct ancestors to the sheela-na-gigs. The clergy of the nineteenth century were always complaining that these images could undermine the power of the church, and it is known that many were handed in after members of the clergy issued threats against those who held them.

A wooden effigy, believed to date back to about 1000 B.C. and made of yew, was found during a peat-cutting session at Ralaghan in County Cavan. It has a deep hole that may either represent the vulva or could have held something that represented a penis, and it was almost certainly regarded as an important cult idol. The original is on display in the National Museum of Ireland in Dublin, and a copy can be seen in the Cavan County Museum. Another fascinating wooden female figure was found at Ballachulish in Lochaber, Scotland, along with the remains of the wickerwork hut in which she was presumably housed, having been preserved in the peat since the early Celtic period, pos-

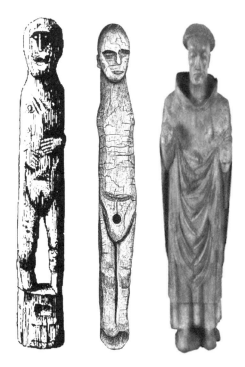

Left and Center: Wooden figures from Ballachulish and Ralaghan. Right: Wooden effigy of Saint Molaise.

sibly as early as the seventh century B.C. The oak figurine, measuring about 1.4 meters in length, had clear sexual organs and frightening facial features, with the eyes inlaid with quartz pebbles. The emphasis on the pudenda suggests that she is a goddess, who, along with her other frightening facial features, appears to have been carved in a similar tradition to the sheela-na-gigs over a thousand years prior to their appearance in the medieval world.

Well-preserved wooden phallic figures dating from the late Bronze Age or early Iron Age have also been found, and it appears that the use of such idols was widespread, as similar figures found preserved in Danish bogs show that this kind of carving probably existed on a much larger scale in Britain and Ireland.

It is known that the tradition of carving wooden images continued into and beyond the Middle Ages. The majority of these were wooden idols, which were semi-Christianized as saints and were being carried around the countryside largely to perform cures. One instance that has survived is the thirteenth-century wooden statuette of Saint Gobnait at Ballyvourney, detailed in Chapter 3, which is still being used for its healing power, but there were others that have been lost or destroyed in recent times. Apart from Saint Gobnait's statue, there are wooden images of Saint Máel Ruain, Bishop of Tallaght, Saint Molua of Killaloe, and Saint Mocheallóg of Kilmallock (Cill Mocheallóg), while the wooden figure of Saint Molaise of Inishmurray in County Sligo is one of the best preserved, having miraculously survived after being thrown overboard from a boat. It is now on display in the National Museum of Ireland, and there is a copy in Sligo Cathedral.

In the nineteenth century, the antiquarian researcher John Windele observed that the Ballyvourney figure was attacked by the clergy, and in the seventeenth century, a wooden effigy of Saint Mac Dara was recorded as being buried by the Archbishop Malachy O'Queely. A wooden figure of Saint Ibar was held in great esteem on Beg Erin Island, in Wexford Harbour, and until the seventeenth century, the local people swore upon this statue instead of on the Gospel. The figure was destroyed on several occasions, but the people managed to replace each destroyed figure.

In 1539, letters patent under the privy seal were issued "for the suppression of the Irish religious houses and for the destruction of statues that were special centres of devotion." In 1676, a Diocesan order, issued in Ossory and Waterford, commanding "the burning of sheela-na-gigs," provides substantial evidence for the existence of wooden figures similar to the sheela-na-gigs and also substantiates the existence of the name prior to it being used in the mid-1800s. Certainly, some very early wooden statuettes have been discovered

Romanesque doorway with heads, Dysert O'Dea.

through the years, and they may well have some bearing on the matter, if only as archaic images that have continued within traditional consciousness.

It would appear from the evidence that, traditionally, wood seems to have been the preferred medium for creating sacred idols. It seems highly probable, therefore, that the sheela-na-gigs were based on original wooden figures long since destroyed, while only the stone images survived.

Although the sheela-na-gigs are undoubtedly late medieval, their features suggest an awareness of pagan imagery. Pre-Romanesque stone figures, such as those from Boa Island, White Island, and Carndonagh, are all connected to ancient monasteries and show that there were likely native prototypes for the sheela-na-gigs since the early Christian period. The combination of the squatting posture and the exposure of the vulva can be traced back through a number of figures carved out of stone, wood, ivory, and other materials since the Celtic Iron Age, which must surely illustrate the descent of the motif from pagan to Christian settings.

Around the start of the second millennium A.D., it appears that there was a sudden reawakening to the "monumental and immortal power of stone," which during the next few centuries manifested itself in the widespread building of churches, round towers, and high crosses. The impetus for the flowering of the sheela-na-gigs may have occurred due to this move toward the permanency of stone and the corresponding Romanesque movement, which was also largely responsible for encouraging the trend of elaborate decoration and the carving of figures in stone.

CHAPTER EIGHT

THE MYSTERIOUS ORIGINS OF THE SHEELA-NA-GIGS

SHEELA-NA-GIGS are the last of an ancient lineage of female goddess figures in this particular state of display that can be traced back to the very dawn of human history. There are a few uncertain links in the chain, but a direct line can be traced from ancient times right through to the Middle Ages. Exactly when the first of these images appears is uncertain, but female imagery and symbolism are universally found at nearly all the rock art sites in Europe and throughout the painted caves from the earliest phase of the Paleolithic or Early Stone Age, about 40,000 years ago.

One of the commonest images is the symbol of the vulva or yoni, and it appears alone or in conjunction with more complete female forms, on rock faces and loose stones. Most of the earlier female forms, however, do not accentuate the vulva. The famous Venus of Laussel figure is typically depicted in the style of the fecund mother goddess but with little or no emphasis on the vulva. Uniquely, she is shown holding a crescent-shaped object in her right hand with thirteen notches that Alexander Marshak and others have consid-

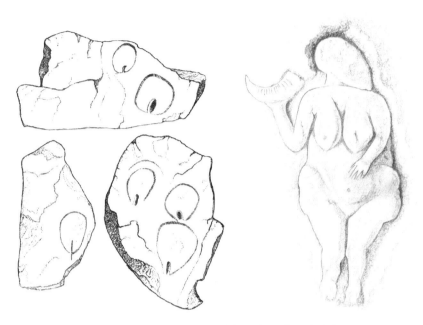

Left: Vulva symbols, a common motif throughout the Paleolithic era.
Right: The "Venus" of Laussel.

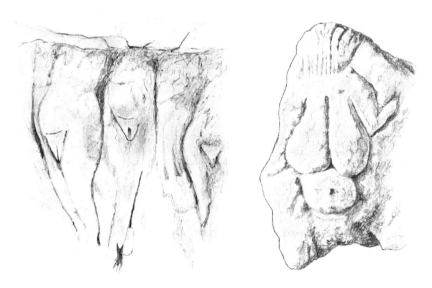

Left: The torsos of three female images, Roc-aux-Sorciers.
Right: Female figure with arm raised, Laussel .

ered to represent a lunar year of thirteen lunations. The two other female figures found in the Laussel cave are less known, one of which is depicted holding an object in her right hand and the other with her left arm raised. Figures like these from the earliest phase of the Palaeolithic era seem to set a traditional form of the rotund female that predominated throughout the whole prehistoric era.

Female figure holding object in her hand, Laussel.

In the Magdalenian culture, between 15,000 and 17,000 years ago, the first known depiction of the triple goddess appeared on a rock face at the entrance to the cave of Roc-aux-Sorciers in Vienne, France. Three female forms float mysteriously into the rock ceiling, headless and without breasts but deliberately emphasizing the abdomen and with clearly defined pudenda carved in relief. As well as the triple goddess carvings, the Roc-aux-Sorciers is famous for its depictions of Ice Age animals and its absence of human male images.

Probably the very earliest example of an image that is depicted in the symbolic/magical stance of the sheela-na-gigs was revealed during excavation of the profoundly important prehistoric site of Göbekli

Female image from Göbekli Tepi.

Fish mother from Lepinski Vir.

Tepe in southeastern Turkey. With her arms and legs set in a classic magical pose, this curious figure could appear as contemporaneous with the medieval sheela-na-gigs, yet it comes from the very earliest megalithic center yet discovered, and dates to the era that marks the end of the Paleolithic and the beginning of the Neolithic or New Stone Age, between 10,000 and 12,000 years ago.

After this, during the Neolithic period, the era that saw the advent of agriculture and a more sedentary way of life, there comes the great explosion of female imagery, with hundreds of so-called "Venus figurines" and female images being created by almost every Eurasian culture. This predominance and diversity of female imagery in prehistory has been well documented by Lithuanian-American archaeologist and anthropologist Marija Gimbutas as well as other researchers. Among the many hundreds of female images from the prehistoric era, however, the symbolism that we see in the sheela-na-gigs, such as the magical postures and explicit genitals, is quite rare.

Perhaps the most compellingly sheela-like figures from the earlier phase of the Neolithic era are the "Fish Mothers" from the sacred sanctuary center of Lepenski Vir, Serbia, on the banks of the Danube River. A number of these figures have been discovered and they date to the pastoral period, the first millennium B.C., while the site itself was in use for several millennia before that. Several of these figures are depicted in a classic pose, with both hands pulling apart a triangular-shaped vulva, and they are unique in that they incorporate elements of an egg, a fish, and a woman, as befits a culture that chose the river for the site of its sacred sanctuary. Some of these are elements of the symbolism of the sheela-na-gigs—the hands holding or pointing to the vulva and such features as striations on the head and body—and sometimes a number of holes have been drilled into them as well, a feature that is seen in a number of sheela-na-gigs.

The shrines of the riverside sanctuary at Lepenski Vir are laid out in a triangular shape, representing the symbolism of the sacred yoni. This triangular shape is a predominant feature of the art of the whole region and has its origins at the same part of the Paleolithic era as other female imagery, while its use persists throughout the whole of the Neolithic period.

Additionally, the great number of female figures that have been unearthed in Malta attest to a widespread devotion to a female deity in the prehistoric era. Although they are almost

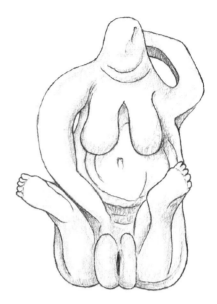

Sheela-like image from Malta.

all created in the traditional form of the rotund or fecund earth mother goddess, there is one clay sculpture that depicts her with one hand reaching down to the vulva and the other pointing to her ear in a typical sheela-na-gig pose. This figure is considered to date from the early Neolithic era, the sixth or seventh millennium B.C., and among hundreds of female images from this culture, it is unique in being the only figure depicted in this pose.

There are very few images considered to have more of a direct connection between the Neolithic sheela-like images and those of the Christian era. One figure that could prove to form this link is an Assyrian bronze figu-

Bronze Assyrian figure, first millennium B.C.

Baubo, first millennium A.D.

Baubo with elaborate headdress.

rine posted on Anthony Weir's website Satan in the Groin: Exhibitionist Figures on Mediæval Churches, which is now in the Pergamon Museum in Berlin. The figure probably dates to the first millennium B.C.

An even closer connection can be made between the sheela-na-gigs and a particular figurine that appears repeatedly in the first centuries of the Christian era. These are small statuettes of naked females known as Baubos, named after the Greek goddess of mirth, and they are often depicted in the typical magical stance of the medieval sheela-na-gig. They appear to have been connected with childbirth and/or the promotion of fertility, for they are mostly found near or within "women's rooms" in houses of the Nile Delta and Alexandria areas that date to the Greek-Egyptian/Hellenistic period. Most importantly, they date from the first to the third centuries, the period when Christianity was emerging from its obscure Middle Eastern origins, and in the very place where the Bible and other religious works were being transcribed into Greek for the first time.

It was the Egyptologist Margaret Murray who, in the 1930s, first noted the similarity between the Baubo figurines and the sheela-na-gigs. Murray was primarily an anthropologist and one of the earliest women to carry out research into the female aspects of earlier cultures. To her, the sheela-na-gigs represented clear evidence of the survival of goddess-oriented beliefs into the later Christian age, and she considered that the image of Baubo was a major influence on the later sheela-na-gig images.

Along with much of early Christian iconography, Baubo is derived from the Egyptian myth of Isis, who is also thought to be related to the goddess Bau of Sumerian legend. According to a Greek legend, when Isis was mourning for her son Osiris, Baubo assumed the posture of exposing herself, and the shock of the display made Isis laugh and cease from lamenting.

The fact that there is only this one popular reference to Baubo in writings existing from ancient times gives the impression that her cult was destroyed and buried under the stampede of various conquests, although there is mention of later erotic rites carried out in her honor. Murray believed that the sheela-na-gigs were worshipped in the same way as the Baubo figures—that is, exclusively by women—and that men were rigorously excluded from these rites. In her usual uninhibited fashion, Murray then went on to express the belief that they played a role in teaching women the pleasures of sex. Such views did little to endear her to the scholarly world, and it is no surprise that her ideas have largely been ignored.

Despite any speculative interpretations by Murray, the Baubo phenomenon constitutes the most tangible connection between the ancient world and the development of the medieval sheela-na-gigs. As is outlined in Chapter 3, there is a very strong connection between the world in which the Baubo figurines were created and the Gaelic/Celtic world, especially Ireland, through the Coptic roots of Christianity in these northwestern lands. There was a connection between the two regions, whether directly with Egypt or, as some scholars suggest, through a connecting route that brought the ancient Gnostic teachings to the British Isles through Europe via France or Spain.

If Baubo traveled directly into Ireland through those early druidic students of Christianity, this would circumvent the need for a Romanesque origin of the figure, and although Baubo herself might have influenced the exhibitionist figures found on those tenth- and eleventh-century churches, they could well have been introduced by Irish monks, many of whom were engaged in establishing monastic communities across Europe in the early Christian era.

More recently, Anthony Weir discovered a figure that could be a crucial link in the chain of development of the sheela-na-gig image. Small clay figures that are clearly modeled on the Baubo image were apparently being carved in France during the Roman occupation period. Weir suggests that such evidence illustrates where the Romanesque artists could easily have derived their inspiration, but it could also indicate a route by which it arrived directly into the lands of the Gaels and Celts.

Weir and James Jerman, the authors of *Images of Lust*, also allowed for the possibility of a link between Baubo and the later medieval manifestation of the exhibiting woman. Because they were mainly using clerical sources to substantiate their ideas on the purpose of the sheela-na-gigs, the connection they made was through the records relating to the early Christian cleric Clement of Alexandria (150 to 215 A.D.), who is said to have been initiated into certain Hellenistic cults around the time when many of the Baubo figures were created.

It is known that Clement's work was still highly influential during the eleventh and twelfth centuries and later via Byzantine writer and historian Michael Psellos (1018–1078). The existence of three female figures on medieval churches in northern Italy, shown "lifting their robes to reveal their private parts, as described by Clement," insinuate that these Baubo figures were known for centuries after Clement died.

Coincidentally, the Eleusinian Mysteries—rites associated with the Hellenistic cult of Persephone and Demeter, to which

Clay Baubo, Roman-era France.

Left: female figure formerly above gateway in Milan.
Right: Hellenistic statue from Alexandria, first–second millennium A.D.

the Baubo myth is related (Demeter being the Greek pantheon's equivalent of Isis)—involved the drinking of a special intoxicating beverage made of barley and pennyroyal. This practice echoes the traditions associated with the Irish goddess Meave or Mebh, who is known as the "intoxicating one." Weir and Jerman also note that the later Greek name for Baubo was Iambé, a name that is still used to describe a hag in parts of Greece, much as sheela-na-gig is still used in Ireland into the present century.

Sheela-like statue, Dubrovnik.

Such an omnipotent archetype as the displaying female probably has the power to reemerge at any time, and examples of exhibiting females have been noted from many places, seemingly unconnected with the western European tradition. One example is the exhibiting female over a spring well on the old town wall of Dubrovnik, Croatia, probably dating from the Roman period but possibly later.

A female figure displayed in this way often has associations with death, such as among some Iroquois tribes in North America, and many Oceanic tribes commonly still use the displayed female as an apotropaic symbol, rather than a fertility symbol, as can be seen by the use of the motif on items such as shields and the stems of canoes. Throughout India, yogic statues of the great goddess Kali still appear at the doorways of Hindu temples, where visitors lick a finger and touch the yoni, the most revered of sacred icons, for luck. In the older Indo-European traditions, the yoni is believed to be the center of divine power, and an image of the displayed woman is associated with the erotic and serpentine energy of tantric beliefs.

Several authors, such as the renowned researcher Marija Gimbutas, have added the sheela-na-gigs to their overview of the place of the feminine in sacred art and of the universality of the female deity. A 2016 book by Starr Goode, *Sheela na Gig: The Dark Goddess of Sacred Power*, delves deeply into the mysterious correlation between the sheela-na-gigs and images from various cultures worldwide. While this is an area of research that could still be expanded upon, this work has confined itself to figures that may be directly relevant to the development of the sheela-na-gigs.

THE SCANDINAVIAN CONNECTION

Because of the Norman/Viking connection with the age when sheela-na-gigs appear on the churches of Britain and Ireland, there has been much speculation that the image may have its ori-

gins in Scandinavia. There is, however, little evidence of this, apart from a very few sheela-like images and the fact that the hierarchy in many parts of the region was traditionally matriarchal, similar to that of the Gaelic/Celtic lands. There exist only a small number of examples from which one could construct a lineage for the sheela-na-gigs having emanated from Scandinavia. However, there are some very curious examples of a tradition that may be in some way related.

Picture stone, Lagnö.

Exhibiting female, Stikelstad.

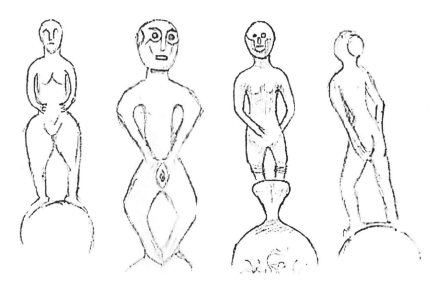

Wooden spoons, Östersund.

One of the better-known examples is the fourth-century picture stone from Lagnö, an ancient pagan center in Södermanland in central Sweden, on which an image of a female figure with her legs spread apart is shown. The area is famous for the number of runic picture stones, yet this is the only example depicting a female entity. The lack of similar images in the vicinity suggests it is a singular or rare instance, rather than a commonly used motif.

Built in 1180, the Romanesque church of Stiklestad in Trøndelag County, Norway, is said to have a sheela-like figure quite high up on the east-facing wall. The figure, however, appears to be wearing a crown, which questions what it's really meant to represent. The village of Stiklestad is home to the Stiklestad National Culture Center, located just across the street from the church, and has very significant historical associations.

However, in the museum in Östersund, in central Sweden, there are some artifacts that suggest an affinity with the sheela-na-gig tradition that survived into the relatively recent historical era. In an exhibition of local folk art are examples of what are known as "wedding spoons," including wooden spoons with images of naked women carved on their handles. The carvings are, however, remarkably sheela-like in the poses, with one even holding her hands fore and aft in the classic pose of several of the Irish sheela-na-gigs and, of course, the Baubo figures.

Unfortunately, little is known about the tradition, other than the examples in the museum, which date to the eighteenth and nineteenth centuries and are thought to have been carved as tokens and given to women by suitors. It may be of significance that the lakes around Östersund were considered special places reserved for royal burials. Some of these burials are of male chieftains, but the richest graves have

Figure on medieval font, Gelsted.

been those of the real rulers of the Viking world, the queens, whose tombs regularly contain rare treasures from far-off lands.

The Danish researcher Klaus Aarsleff has researched examples of non-Christian art in Scandinavia, and his book *Troldsten i Guds Hus* includes pictures of one female figure carved on the base of a baptismal font in the eleventh- or twelfth-century church in Gelsted. The serpentine imagery surrounding the figure suggests a similarity to the Lagnö figure, but the way her hands are positively aimed toward the vulva more clearly connects her to the sheela-na-gigs.

IRELAND, LAND OF THE GODDESS

Ireland has a unique heritage that can be traced back to the Mesolithic era or Middle Stone Age and is most famous for its many thousands of very early megalithic monuments that, after thousands of years, can still be found in every part of the landscape. In the latter part of the twentieth century, the greatest of these ancient monuments, the passage mounds of the Boyne Valley (Brú na Bóinne in Irish), underwent extensive investigation, which has brought to

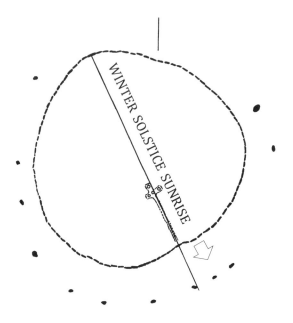

WINTER SOLSTICE SUNRISE

Plan of the great womb mound of Newgrange.

light the full majesty of Ireland's ancient cultural heritage. This site with its womb-like mounds is regarded as the birthplace of the goddesses and gods of the ancient world, and the sacred landscape upon which they stand is dedicated to the primary mother goddess Bóande, mentioned in previous chapters, who is also the cow goddess. Newgrange, the largest of the mounds, is primarily a monument to fertility, designed to symbolically give birth to the sun god Aengus on an annual basis by allowing a beam of light from the primary heavenly deity, the Grianan Mór (the Great Sun), to penetrate and fertilize the womb/mound of the mother goddess Bóande.

Such symbolic mythology, having its origins 5,000 to 6,000 years ago, has influenced all subsequent cultural development on the island until relatively recent times. It forms an underlying cultural tradition that has a fundamental belief in the ultimate power of the feminine. It is, after all, a land that has always been named after one of three goddesses: Banba, Fódla, and currently the Goddess Ériu.

That this belief in the power of the feminine lasted right up to the very end of Gaelic/Celtic culture in the 1600s is the essential message left to us in the sheela-na-gigs. Yet despite that goddesses and hags in various forms dominate both mythology and folk tradition, there is virtually no tradition of representing the female form until the sheela-na-gigs appear. In fact, there is a total absence of representational imagery until the Celts introduced stylistic animal and human forms as a part of the art forms in the latter half of the first millennium B.C. Prior to that, all art is purely symbolic and consists of spirals, circles, and various established patterns, as exemplified in the megalithic art of the great passage mounds of the Brú na Bóinne.

Celtic Christians of the Middle Ages were steeped in these old mythologies, yet they lacked a tradition of depicting anything but the most stylistic and symbolic images. Baubo, or imagery derived from Baubo, such as is found in the Romanesque carvings, may well have been the original inspiration to which they added their deeper symbolic understanding of the eternal deities. Thereby, ostensibly, they developed the mysterious sacred sheela-na-gigs, in their various forms, in the image of Bóande, the great ancestral mother of the goddesses and gods, and the many goddesses that inhabited the consciousness of the people of this ancient land.

Bronze Baubo.

A CATALOGUE AND GUIDE TO THE SHEELA-NA-GIGS OF IRELAND

IT IS CURRENTLY KNOWN that there are, or were, at least 118 Sheela-na-gigs on the island of Ireland. This is not an exact figure, since there are records of figures that may have been Sheela-na-gigs, and a growing awareness of them that means that new figures are regularly being revealed.

It is known that at least fourteen are known only from earlier records, having gone missing since an account was made of them, and there are twelve of which there is no record of their origin.

The original locations of the known Sheela-na-gigs are almost equally divided between those that originate from either a church or other religious structure, and those that were erected on castles or other medieval buildings such as town walls.

In the Guide each entry is annotated with the following:

In Situ: Still on the site, but not necessarily in its original position.

Missing: Known only from earlier records but fairly positively identified as a Sheela-na-gig.

The map shows the locations of those figures that are still on or close to the places where they originated. Many of the Sheela-na-gigs are located on private property; visiting them is at the discretion of the landowner.

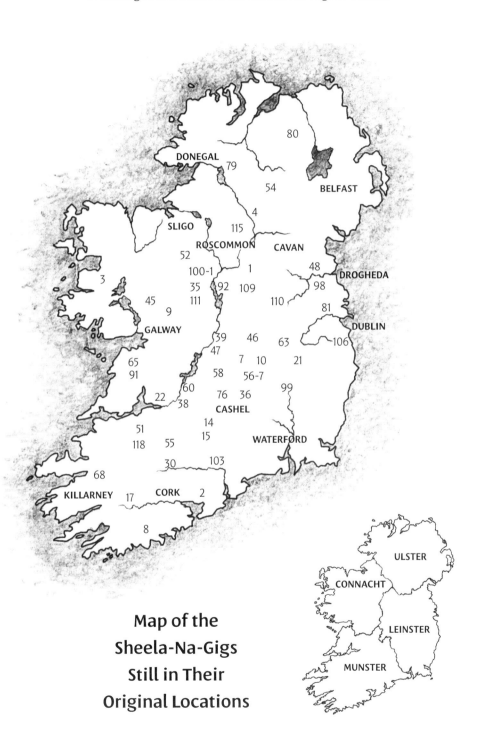

Map of the
Sheela-Na-Gigs
Still in Their
Original Locations

MUNSTER
County Cork

2. AGHADOE — In Situ / On Dovecote

Aghadoe is approximately 1.5 mi / 2 km north of Killeagh village, which is approximately 30 km east of Cork city on the N25.

This well-preserved Sheela-na-gig has been re-erected on the old dovecote, which is all that remains of the castle. It has been carved in high relief and is very well preserved with defined linear strokes across her arms and legs, accentuated ribbing, four small centrally placed breasts and clearly defined genital features. The raised hand holds the rather indistinct form of a pointed object, and there are strange nodules very clearly carved into the wrists, three on her downward-pointing right arm which reaches toward the vulva and at least two but possibly originally three on her upraised left arm. 40 x 30 cm.

8. BALLINACARRIGA — In Situ / On Castle

The castle is situated about 4 mi / 7 km southeast of Dunmanway and should be signposted from both the Bandon and the Clonakilty roads. This well-preserved Sheela-na-gig is located quite high up on the east facing wall of the castle, to the right of and above the main entrance door. The right hand passes beneath the thigh whilst her left hand passes on top of the other thigh in a classic pose. One eye is open while the other is just a slit and what looks like a lunar crescent encircles her eye. Two vertical bands are deliberately carved on the upper part of the figure and the breasts are shown at an angle.

The upper floor, on the level where the Sheela-na-gig is situated, was used as a chapel until the last century and is renowned for its decorated stones depicting religious motifs. The castle is a listed National Monument and a key should be available in the disused Castle Bar close to the castle. Approx 45 x 30 cm.

15. BALLYNAMONA —Missing

Ballynamona Castle stands on the banks of the little Awbeg river about 5 mi / 8 km southeast of Mallow. It was apparently built into a gate pier, until around 1820 when a mason carrying out repairs destroyed the figure, 'on account of its characteristics.' Later it was found some distance away from the castle 'but so smashed up that she was beyond repair.' She is recorded as a talisman of the Nagles who built the castle, and it was said by locals that 'it is certain that once she left her place in the castle the Nagles did not long survive her.'

17. BALLYVOURNEY —In Situ / Over Church Window

Ballyvourney is about 9 mi / 15 km west of Macroom on the main road to Killarney road. St. Gobnait's church or Abbey is signposted on the left a short distance before you reach the village. This very small benign Sheela-na-gig can be found carved into an oval recess at an odd angle on a lintel, which has been reused and set at a slant over a window on the south wall of the church. The hands point toward her lower abdomen or genital area, and although the legs are missing the figure appears to be standing. The site is an important pilgrimage center and the practice of rubbing the figure is still part of the rounds at the church. In the 1930s it was recorded that the Sheela-na-gig was regarded as an actual image of St. Gobnait, and to many still is. It is only 18 cm tall.

17. BARNAHEALY—Missing

This figure is said to have been found in the ruins of Barnahealy or Castle Warren, to the southwest of Ringaskiddy but has since gone missing. In the late 1800s the antiquarian Windele, who was very familiar with the representation of the Sheela-na-gig, recorded that 'a brown gritty stone with a rude representation of a female figure in nudibus.'

30. CASTLE WIDENHAM—In Situ / Private

Castle Widenham is just west of Castletownroche on the Fermoy–Mallow road. In the mid-1800s this figure was recorded as lying by a Holy Well situated on the banks of the Awbeg River, but in 1906 it was found in a backwater where it had been thrown. It was subsequently re-erected by the well, but in 1934 it was recorded as having again disappeared into 'the rank vegetation' and was rescued then set up by the tower of the nearby castle. More recently it was removed to the safe indoor environment of the castle and can only be seen by permission of the owner.

The Sheela-na-gig is carved onto a large slab of rock with a lean torso, no indication of breasts, and hands point to clearly shown pudenda. There is a curious 'headdress' with snippets down both sides of the head. Local tradition relates that the figure was frequently touched for help in childbirth and according to the *Ordnance Survey Field Book* of the late nineteenth century it is stated that the figure was 'bearing an image supposed to be that of a Saint,' so the original saint to whom the well was dedicated was most certainly not Patrick. It looks as if it was originally a set laid down on a quoin stone.

59. GLANWORTH — In Storage

Found in the course of an archaeological dig beneath a layer of rubble in a vaulted ground-floor chamber of the gate tower and appears to have been deliberately hidden here sometime in the late seventeenth century. The figure is sculpted in deep relief, and having been pre-served from weathering such small details are still very clearly defined. Both hands meet at the vulva with the left arm passing over the left thigh while the right arm passes under the right thigh, and the anus is clearly represented. The castle was originally built in the thirteenth century by the de Caunteton or Condon family and is built entirely of limestone, whereas the Sheela-na-gig is sculpted in the round from red sandstone and would have stood out clearly from her position on the castle walls. At present, this figure is kept in the Heritage Department Storeroom in Mallow, at the rear of the Garda Station. 52 cm x 35 cm.

95. RINGASKIDDY — Fitzgerald's Park Museum

This is one of two Sheela-na-gigs kept in Fitzgerald's Museum in Cork city. In the mid-1980s a figure was retrieved from a garden of a deserted

house near the village and was subsequently acquired by the museum. The Sheela-na-gig has a disproportionately large head with arms hanging down; a long, slender body; almost straight legs; and both hands are directed toward a slit indicating the vulva. She is one of the unusual types with inward-turned feet. It is quite probable that this figure is one of the two Sheela-na-gigs that were recorded as once having existed in a private garden at Ringaskiddy in the early years of this century but were not available during visits by Guest in 1934 and 1935. The second figure may have been the one from Tracton.

116. TRACTON—Fitzgerald's Park Museum

Also kept in the Fitzgerald's Museum is a figure found in a garden on the site of the ruined Tracton Abbey, a Cistercian establishment founded in 1224. The Sheela-na-gig and a few other stones are all that remains of the former religious center. Guest thought that the stone on which the figure is carved had originally formed part of the jamb of a window or door and is contemporary with its construction. It was included in Guest's list of 1935 and again by Andersen who noted her 'quaintly carved pudenda.' The arms hang parallel to the torso but do not touch it. A band-like feature partly across the flank of the figure is an unusual feature. 36 x 30 cm.

County Tipperary

11. BALLYFINBOY — In Situ / On Castle
The castle stands close to the Ballyfinboy River about 1 mi / 2 km west of Borrisokane. This Sheela-na-gig is known locally as the Dancer and currently the best directions are to follow signs for the Dancer B&B. This is the local name for the figure. It is an early tower house, possibly thirteenth–fourteenth century, which means that it is now mostly in ruins and that which still stands is unstable. The Sheela-na-gig is considered contemporary with its construction. She is situated about 10 ft / 3 m above the ground at the height where the batter of the lower wall ends. The hands pass below the thighs and meet around the middle of the abdomen, which is slightly sagging.

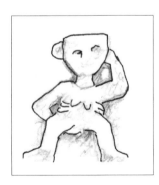

13. BALLYNACLOGH — In Situ / On Church
The Sheela-na-gig is on a quoin stone on the southwestern corner of the church.
Ballynaclogh is about 3 mi / 5 km southeast of Nenagh on the R498, the Borrisoleigh road. The church is next to a T junction in the village and is thought to date to the mid-fifteenth century. Hands and arms similar to Behy in Sligo but she is otherwise a very different type of figure; her ribs are clearly depicted, and the large head gives an impish look. The figure is within reach of the ground and has suffered damage to her lower portion. Basically she has been sanitized by the removal of that part of her that someone obviously found offensive.

14. BALLYNAHINCH—In Situ / On Castle
Ballynahinch castle is about 2.5 mi / 4 km west of Cashel but close to the west bank of the river Suir on its northern side. The Sheela-na-gig is situated about 20 ft / 6 m from the ground on the main tower, over the door, and may be difficult to see. It was said to have come from the ruins of a church a short distance to the north of the castle. The hands are joined above the pudenda and the legs are widely splayed. The head is large and round, the eyes have pupils clearly marked and there are billowy lines across the forehead. 60 cm.

23. BURGESBEG I—National Museum
There are two Sheela-na-gigs thought to have originated from the old church of Burgesbeg, about 7 mi / 10 km west of Nenagh. This figure was found in 1932 by Mr. Wallace inside the church at the base of the wall of the only remaining gable, and he believed it formed part of an arch of either a door or a window. Carved in relief, it has two round balls, presumably the breasts, low down on the abdomen while the vulva which is deeply hollowed out, perhaps rubbed. 71 x 38 cm.

24. BURGESBEG II—In Storage
This is presumed to be the second figure from Burgesbeg. In her very brief article in 1939, 'A Sheela-na-gig at Clonmacnoise,' Edith Guest stated, 'Mr. Wallace has informed me of the finding of two Sheela-na-gigs found lying outside the south wall of Burgesbeg churchyard.' The figure is currently kept in a store room adjoining the cathedral at Clonmacnoise and has bent legs, bulbous eyes and clearly defined ribs.

28. CASHEL I—In Situ / On Religious Building

There are three Sheela-na-gigs in Cashel, one on The Rock, and two within the town. Thousands of visitors to this famous historical site pass each year beneath a reclining Sheela-na-gig carved on a quoin stone on the southeast corner of the 'Hall of the Vicar's Choral.' This is a fifteenth-century building said to have housed the clergy and is now the visitor's reception center and museum.

The figure is squatting with hands reaching down from the front and the back. O'Donovan referred to it as 'the Idol,' but he may well have been referring to a figure with a cat-like head, rotund belly and intertwining legs known also as the 'Cat Goddess' that was previously regarded as a Sheela-na-gig and can now be seen inside the museum (see Appendix). Local tradition also refers to a Sheela-na-gig here that was said to have had the power to avert the Evil Eye but this also may have been referring to the Cat Goddess.

The Rock of Cashel was a place of great religious and political importance, the royal residence of the Kings of Munster until 1101 A.D. when King Muirchertach O'Brian gave it to the Church.

29. CASHEL II—In Situ / In Cashel Palace Hotel

This figure was found at the rear of Cashel Palace Hotel on a section of old wall. It is now on display inside the Hotel. The figure is rather worn and indistinct and some thoughtful person has made a rubbing, which helps clarify the image.

40. CLONMEL — National Museum

Acquired by the National Museum in 1944 after being discovered in the wall of a bank opposite the site of a former Dominican Priory. The figure became known as the 'Idol of Blue Anchor Lane,' in reference to the place where she was discovered. She is depicted seated with thighs splayed, with the right hand passing underneath the thighs and touching the genitals. The lean ribs are carved in relief, and a heavy pattern of parallel lines is clearly delineated as well as striations on the breasts. There are two curious holes, one to the left of vulva and one in position of anus, and the top half of her face is partly destroyed or badly weathered. 62 x 36 cm.

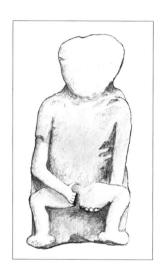

41. CLONOULTY — Bolton Library, Cashel

This figure was found buried up to her neck at the foot of a yew tree in the course of a cleaning-up scheme of Clonoulty Church in January 1989. The age of the yew tree indicates that the stone was buried at least sometime prior to 1800 and is thought to have been placed in this position as a marker, possibly of a grave, or maybe the Sheela-na-gig. Unfortunately the face has been so damaged that virtually no features survive.

Fortunately, the rest of the figure is not so badly damaged, and can be seen to have been sculpted in deep relief with rib marks showing and clear indications of striations along the side of her head and neck. Clonoulty is the site of a former Preceptory (temple) of the Knight's Templars and was the wealthiest of their Irish foundations. The figure is now located in the G.P.A. Bolton Library in Cashel. 70 x 35 cm.

56. FETHARD I—In Situ, On Town Wall

There are two Sheela-na-gigs in the old medieval town of Fethard and another two in Kiltinane 2.2 mi/ 3.5 km to the south (68–69).

This has to be one of the most startling Sheela-na-gigs and can be found on a section of the old fourteenth-century town wall overlooking the medieval bridge over the Clashawley River at the entrance to the medieval walled town of Fethard. Although the figure is strategically located facing the old entry into the town, she blends in with the rest of the wall and is only really visible from quite close up. Certainly this is one of the few examples that could truly be described as ugly or frightening with her emaciated look, very noticeable incised ribs, striated chevron pattern on the left cheek and her neck, and a large growth on her right ear. Grimly set teeth and large, rimmed staring eyes with pupils add to her hideous appearance. Local researcher James O'Connor commented that 'it must be one of the most powerfully apotropaic of all the figures.'

57. FETHARD II—In Situ / In the Abbey

This very curious figure is situated on the north face of the wall, at the east end of the ancient Augustian Friary. It is possible that it was originally erected upon the earliest church at the Abbey, founded in c. 1300, now in ruins. It is very finely carved with indication of ribs and streaked cheeks and prominent asymmetrical ears. The legs are very thin and widely spaced, and it has been suggested that the lower regions have been hacked as the right hand appears is missing and details below the abdomen are unclear.

60. HOLYCROSS—In Situ

Situated on the river Suir between Cashel and Thurles, Holycross Abbey was originally founded by the Benedictines in the twelfth century and not long after passed on to the Cistercian order. Discovered during restoration work on the Abbey in 1970, it is located on the south wall of the west range about 3 m from the ground on the same side as the entrance to the cloister. Unfortunately it is badly damaged, deliberately hacked away, which is a positive identifier of a true Sheela-na-gig.

69. KILSHANE—In Situ / On Farmhouse

Kilshane House is about halfway along the Tipperary to Bansha road. The Sheela-na-gig is difficult to spot as it is inserted high up on a wall beneath a decorative arch. The farm was originally part of the Holy Ghost Father's Seminary. Figure has large round head and stern appearance, legs spread apart with both hands reaching down to the pudenda.

70. KILTINANE I—Missing

Kiltinan Church is located about 2.2 mi / 3.5 km southeast of Fethard on the R706 road to Carrick on Suir. This curious figure that appears as if dancing or doing a jig was originally erected as a quoin stone, and the image was lying down on the southwest corner of the church. It is one of the figures from which the name entered into common usage after it was described by O'Donovan in the mid-1800s. It was removed from the church by persons unknown on the 9th January 1990. The crime has never been solved and this most important Sheela-na-gig has never been located.

Unusual features include her pipe-stem neck and two nipples on her left breast. An exact replica carved by James O'Connor was to have been erected in place of the original but this has not happened. It is (or was?) one of the largest figures, 81 x 51 cm.

71. KILTINANE II — In Situ / On Well House / Private

Kiltinan Castle, which dates back to 1215, is a short way to the east of Kiltinan Church. This figure, which was called 'the Guardian of the Well,' is now found overlooking the stream on one side of a round, fortified well-house, internally connected with the castle yard. However, this is not its original position but was erected there in 1940.

The figure was first identified in 1840 and described in the Proceedings of the Royal Academy, Dublin as being 'discovered at Kiltinane Castle,' but it is probable that she may have originally been one of the specimens from Kiltinan Church, mentioned in 1909 by the then-owner of the castle, Colonel R. Cooke.

This figure is very important, as she is the only example of a Sheela-na-gig with both arms raised, and one of the few that hold objects in their hands. These objects are subject to various interpretations such as a dagger and a torque or horseshoe, but they may also portray such goddess symbolism as the circle and the serpent.

76. LIATHMORE — In Situ / On Church

The site of this early, seventh-century monastery lies on the south side of the old Cork to Dublin road (now the R639) approximately 6 mi / 9 km from Urlingford. There is a mixture of remains on the site, including the remnants of an 11th- or 12th-century church (the larger of the two churches on the site) on which can be found the Sheela-na-gig. The figure, carved in sandstone, is found on the Romanesque north doorway above a row of pellets. She appears on her side, straight legs, both hands joined around the genital organs, a large triangular head and eyes, and six lobes.

84. MOYCARKEY—Missing

Moycarkey Castle, on the Cashel road about 3 mi / 5 km from Thurles, was described in the last century as having a Sheela-na-gig set in the south wall. A nineteenth-century sketch of the figure in the R.I.A. Library, Dublin, has the caption 'the country people have a legend and call it Cathleen Owen.' According to local lore the figure came from the ruins of a nearby church to bring 'luck about the house.'

86. NEWTOWN-LENNAN—National Museum

Remains of the old church of Newtown-Lennan, reported to incorporate twelfth-century fragments including 'a rude sandstone figure,' can be found about 3.5 mi / 5.6 km north of Carrick on Suir at the foot of the Slievenamon Hills. Subsequently acquired by the National Museum, it is recorded that this very worn Sheela-na-gig was originally found on 'the surface of an ancient churchyard.' 37 x 27 cm.

94. REDWOOD—In Situ / On Castle

Redwood castle should be signposted to the north off the Birr road about 4.5 mi / 7 km from Portumna. The Sheela-na-gig is located about 14 m

above the main doorway, slightly to the right and just underneath the overhanging barbican. She is sculpted in deep relief and has a large head, large eyes, nose and mouth, and a very prominent right ear. The body is long and slender with tiny round breasts and grooves at the sides of the head and body. Her legs are only slightly splayed and she is touching or pulling the pudenda from above.

96. ROCHESTOWN — Missing

This was one of the first Sheela-na-gigs recorded by an antiquarian after being visited by Mr. R.P. Coles in the 1840s, and is one of the two figures from which the name originates. Unfortunately, it is now missing, having disappeared sometime between the late 1800s and Guest's visit to the site in the 1930s. All that remains is a sketch by T.J. Westropp made shortly after its initial discovery. A benign-looking, seated figure with well-defined breasts, knees widely splayed and the right hand clearly touching her pudenda. The old church, in which a Sheela-na-gig was once set in the east gable, can be found about 2.5 mi / 4 km southwest of Cahir.

103. SHANRAHAN — In Situ / On Church

Shanrahan church can be seen on the south side of the road about 4 mi / 6 km east of Ballyporeen on the R665. It is carved in pronounced relief from red sandstone and set very prominently into the west-facing wall of the old church tower, directly over the main entrance. It is difficult to gain a clear view of the finer details but her left leg is turned jauntily outwards with the foot in-turned. A very worn figure that might possibly be a Sheela-na-gig was found in recent years on the eastern wall.

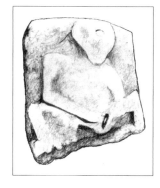

112. THURLES — In Situ / Old Town Wall

The Sheela-na-gig still stands on a surviving section of the old town wall that was probably adjacent to the south town gate near the Black Castle. This is now at the back of a yard on the south side of Liberty Square. The figure is badly worn and many features are unclear, but she can be seen to have widely splayed legs and her right arm reaches down to a well-defined vulva. One eye is still discernible on a triangular-shaped head with characteristic elongated chin, and the left foot appears to be in-turned. The Butlers, Earls of Ormond, created the walled town and dates as early as the twelfth century have been suggested for the construction of the wall, but this section probably dates to the fourteenth century.

County Kerry

68. KILSARKAN — In Situ / On Church Window

Kilsarkan church is about 4 mi / 6.5 km east of Farranafore. The Sheela-na-gig is carved into the lintel of the south window. Both the genital area and several places around the whole window frame are extensively rubbed in a cross pattern with a stone or pebble as part of the rounds. Possibly a relatively late carving, perhaps a contemporary of Ballyvourney or Clenagh. The curious features are the prominent cow-like ears and a strange rope-like headdress, and one leg raised.

77. LIXNAW—National Museum

Lixnaw is about 7 mi / 11 km southwest of Listowel. This figure was acquired by the National Museum in 1964 after being found in a riverbed near 'The Court,' a castle built in 1320 by Baron Lixnaw, from which the figure may originate. She is carved in relief, has small, flat breasts, and her hands pass under thighs to pull apart her pudenda.

93. RATOO—In Situ / On Round Tower

Ratoo Round Tower is about 5 mi / 8 km south of Ballybunion, near the village of Ballyduff. This is the only example of a Sheela-na-gig placed on a Round Tower and the figure is carved on the corner of the high north window, facing inwards. It was discovered in 1880–81 during restoration work and a cast was made of it for the Old Kilkenny Historical Society. Ratoo is one of the finest round towers in Ireland, with a finely carved doorway and various other unusual features.

County Limerick

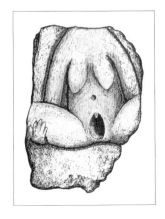

25. CAHERELLY—Hunt Museum Limerick

This sadly headless Sheela-na-gig was found in a culvert near the site of the now-destroyed Caherelly Castle, less than 1.5 mi / 2.5 km north of the well-known prehistoric center of Lough Gur. This was once an important seat of the old Eoghanacht chiefs of the area, who obviously honoured their local female deities. This is an unusually plump figure with the most cavernous vagina of any of the known figures. Usually on display but invariably kept in a badly lit part of the Museum.

51. DUNNAMAN—In Situ / On Castle

Dunnaman Castle is about 2 mi / 3 km northwest of Croom and the castle is now situated within a working dairy farm. This is one of the largest and most overt Sheela-na-gigs in Ireland, as well as one of the best preserved. She exhibits some very interesting details; the figure is set within a frame and has remarkably distinct ribbing on the chest area. There is something protruding from below the vulva similar to some other Sheela-na-gigs that some regard as representing the menstrual flow but which may also refer to the flow of water or a river.

55. FANTSTOWN—In Situ / On Castle

The sixteenth-century castle is situated approx 1.5 mi / 2 km east of Kilmallock and can be seen close to the R515 on the south side of the road. This fine Sheela-na-gig is carved on a quoin stone on the north face of the tower and about 20 ft / 6 m from the ground. Not easy to spot at first; can be seen to be a classic figure with large head, splayed legs, hanging pudenda and hands holding the top of the legs.

118. TULLOVIN—In Situ / On Castle

Tullovin or Tullavin Castle is about 2 mi / 3 km south of Croom on the east side of the R516. The figure is on a quoin stone high on the south face of the peel tower, dated to the late fifteenth century. It is well-preserved, carved in handsome relief in a reclining position. Her left hand points to her head, upon which is a very strange and unusual headdress, and her right hand reaches down behind the thigh to touch the pudenda.

County Clare

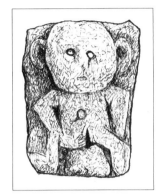

16. BALLYPORTRY—Clare Museum, Ennis

This Sheela-na-Gig, carved in limestone, was found a short way from the late fifteenth- or early sixteenth-century castle which stands right by the Corofin to Gort road about 0.5 mi / 1 km east of Corofin. It was removed to the National Museum in 1942. A very curious figure with an over-large head, deep-set round eyes with pupils, broad shoulders, a large round navel, signs of teeth and possibly an anus. The hands reach behind the thighs and her fingers hold open her vulva, which is depicted in considerable detail. 53 x 38 cm.

22. BUNRATTY—In Situ / In Castle

This is one of Ireland's most famous castles, situated between Shannon Airport and Limerick City. The Sheela-na-gig was originally on the inner reveal of a window at the top of the south-west tower, which dates from the first half of the seventeenth century but during restoration was set into the wall of the 'hall of the great keep.' She appears to be a late example, depicted with eyes set into hollow sockets, bared teeth and widely splayed legs. The arms pass below the legs and make up almost a full circle with the hands placed on the rim of the pudenda. The present castle was built about 1460 and was the seat of the O'Briens, Earls of Thomond until the early eighteenth century.

33. CLENAGH—In Situ / On Castle

The castle, a late sixteenth-century tower house built by the McMahons of Clonderlaw, now

forms part of a large farm close to the western perimeter of Shannon Airport. This curious spindly figure is situated very low down on a quoin stone on the southeast side and appears to be contemporary with the castle. It is almost totally symbolic in form and the squat-legged position is unusual. The pudendum is well defined and indicated by an oblong, diamond-shaped depression which shows signs of rubbing; her head and neck are outlined by a deep groove. 50 x 37 cm.

38. CLONLARA – In Situ / On Bridge

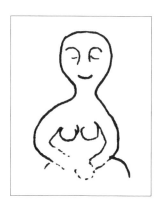

The figure is situated on an old canal bridge at Clonlara about midway between Limerick and Killaloe. A badly worn and damaged figure carved in a similar style to Clenagh castle. Westropp thought it may have come from nearby Newtown Castle which was built in the 1380s, but may also have come from a castle of the Earls of Ormond, since a later Earl was instrumental in building the canal in the mid-1700s and erected this bridge at about the same time as the castle was pulled down.

Known locally as 'The Witches Stone' and also as Peadar Taigdhe Buidhe, it is damaged and the lower section is barely discernible, but earlier researchers found sufficient traces of splayed legs and her right hand probably resting on her right thigh with the left hand on or close to the pubic area. According to Guest (1934) it was said 'to have been defaced by the landowner about three generations ago.' 62 x 47 cm.

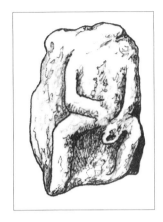

64. KILLALOE — In Situ / On Holy Well

This headless figure is placed over St. Flannan's Holy Well opposite the Romanesque church dedicated to the same saint, and it is thought that the Sheela-na-gig may have originally been erected on the church. The well is in a small garden at the rear of a branch of the Bank of Ireland so access is restricted, but one would trust she is at least in safe keeping from further damage. The breasts can still be discerned and the knees are widely splayed with the hands meeting above the thighs in a gesture toward the pudenda.

65. KILLINABOY — In Situ / On Church

Killinaboy is easily located as it is less than 2 mi / 3 km northwest of Corofin on the R467 road to Kilfenora. The church can be seen on a low rise on the right very close to the road where there is even a large parking space with a map and information about the many archaeological and historical sites in the area.

This is a very unique church built on the site of an early monastery founded by the mysterious figure of St. Inghean Bhaoithe, and the Sheela-na-gig here is probably one of the most important examples in the country. The figure is most prominently displayed directly above the entrance door to the church, which confirms the central importance of the image. It is carved in deep relief but is unfortunately becoming rather worn with age and there is a dire need for some thought to its preservation.

The ribs and incised folds of the neck are still visible in a good light, and hands meet in a gesture toward the vulva, below which is something like a tail or the kind of mysterious extrusion seen on figures such as the Ballinderry Sheela-na-gig (Galway 9). See Also Chapter 4.

91. RATH (Rathblathmaic) — In Situ / On Church

This former monastic site, named after another mysterious saint, St. Blathmac, is about 2 mi / 3 km southeast of Corofin and just under 1 mi / 1.5 km north of Dysert O'Dea. Both sites are signposted in the area. The remains of the old nave and chancel date from various periods, and this little Sheela-na-gig is on an ornamented panel of a lower window lintel that has been inserted upside down on the south side of the interior wall. See also Chapter 3.

Lidar image courtesy of Gary Dempsey, Digital Heritage Age.

LEINSTER
County Wexford

67. KILMOKEA — National Museum

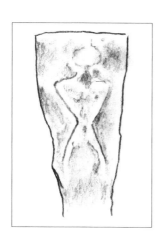

An unusual figure can be found on the reverse side of a gravestone. It is thought that the stone may have originated from Dunbrody Abbey. An unusual figure of indeterminate date, obviously styled as a Sheela-na-gig type figure and possibly seventeenth-century, thus antedating the main period of Sheela-na-gig carving but within the era when memory of their original function would probably have still existed.

County Kilkenny

10. BALLEEN LITTLE – In Situ / On Wall

The site of this castle is about 2.5 mi / 4 km northwest of Freshford to the west of the L1804. The figure is thought to have originated from a castle that is now no longer on the site and which is said to have been built on the site of an earlier church. The Sheela-na-gig is currently inserted into a wall at the rear of a farmhouse built on the site of the castle. The features of this Sheela-na-gig are quite well preserved: facial striations that give it a cat-like look, deep ribbing, and the mouth clearly displaying gritted teeth. Freitag noted a plait-like band that hangs from the left ear. 45 x 52 cm.

12. BALLYLARKIN- National Museum

This is one of the finest examples of the extraordinary art of carving Sheela-na-gigs, and originates from the thirteenth-century parish church of Ballylarkin, less than 2 mi / 3 km southwest of Freshford. The church is a good example of the style of this relatively early period though partly ruinous and it is unknown exactly where the figure was originally located. It is probably fortunate that it was removed to the National Museum in Dublin where it is kept in good preservation.

It is undoubtedly one of the most refined Sheela-na-gig images, with unusually clear facial features and a yogic-like pose, with one finger of the left hand delicately touching the pudenda and the right hand resting on the knee. She appears to have two pairs of breasts though the lower feature may be ribbing. 58 x 32 cm.

36. CLOMANTAGH—In Situ / On Castle

Clomantagh, or Croomantagh, castle, can be found on R693, the Urlingford to Kilkenny road, on the north side of the road about 3 mi / 5 km from Freshford. The Sheela-na-gig is situated at a height of approximately 8 m on a southwest quoin stone of the castle in a reclining position. She is quite a large figure with big feet and set within a recessed frame, which follows the contours of her body. Her right hand is raised up toward her face and her left hand is clearly depicted touching her pudenda. On her left-hand side only is a raised slender band, which stems from the side of her head to the side of her body. The stone on which she is carved appears to be of a slightly darker grey than the rest of the stone used to build the castle.

43. COOLIAGH MORE—Roth House, Kilkenny

This Sheela-na-gig was unearthed during clearance work on Cooliagh Church near Kells Priory. Local tradition relates that the figure was found in a well at Kyle and brought to Cooliagh churchyard early in the twentieth century. There is speculation it could have derived from a pre-Norman church, but could have originated in the ancient monastic site of Kilree with its old church and a round tower. The left hand of the figure appears to rest on the thigh and the right hand is clearly gesturing toward the genitals. The position of the feet is unusual in that while the left leg is outstretched with the foot inclined toward the left, the right leg is bent tightly at the knee and there are traces of ribbing on the chest. Lidar image by Gary Dempsey, Digital Heritage Age.

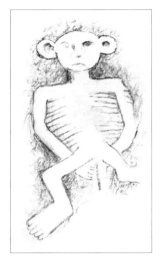

117. TULLAROAN—Private

This large and extraordinary figure was discovered around 2006 while clearing the rubble from an old school; the original location is unknown. It is very well preserved with tool marks clearly visible. Features such as the ribbing are very clear, and she lacks breasts. The short left leg and enlarged right foot are unique features, while the vulva is depicted by a long deep groove. Tullaroan is about 8 mi / 13 km west of Kilkenny, and the Sheela-na-gig is kept by Noel Coogan 2 km along the Freshford road from Tullaroan on the right side of the road. 73 x 62 cm.

County Offaly

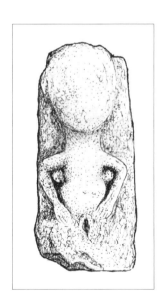

20. BIRR—National Museum

This figure was acquired by the National Museum in 1956, and although its exact former location is not recorded, it likely originated from St. Brendan's church. It is a curious but badly worn Sheela-na-gig with small hands reaching down toward the abdomen. Small, round breasts are located under her arms, and the fact that her neck and head are rolled backwards is an odd feature. It has been suggested that the stone on which the figure is carved is really a broken-off corbel and what is the apparent top of the stone would have been the front and the rest of her body would have been facing downwards. 53 x 30 cm.

34. CLOGHAN—Missing

A figure was reported as originating from the castle at Lusmagh, on the river Brosna, a short way south of Banagher. In a report of 1906, a local landowner, Mr. Cooke, stated that he had in his possession an image, 'called by the peasantry the witch,' that was carved out of limestone. He supposed that the figure represented 'an hermaphrodite, one of the breasts being like the sun and the other a crescent like the moon.' It was said to be 'preserved in a museum in the south of Ireland,' but there is no record of its existence. The description strongly suggests that he was describing a Sheela-na-gig.

37. CLONBULLOGE—Clonbulloge Library

This unique legless figure was discovered in the 1970s in the Figile River below Kilcumber Bridge, near Clonbulloge. The figure is carved into the corner of a limestone quoin in high relief and is deliberately depicted without legs. Large hands pull open the vulva, and the clitoris is clearly defined. Striations on the forehead and left cheek are clearly delineated and the right cheek appears to have a bump or growth. Other pieces of decorated stone found in the river suggest the destruction of a medieval building in the locality but the lack of any nearby castle leaves doubt over the origin of these remnants. The figure is now kept in the local public library.

39. CLONMACNOISE—In Situ / On Church

This early figure can be found on the Romanesque doorway of the 'Nun's Chapel' within the former 'Enclosure of the Abbess,' around 500 m to

the north of the main complex at Clonmacnoise. It is inside the little church on the interior side of the decorated chancel arch on the seventh voussoir on the left. It is carved in typical Romanesque style with various other faces and animal heads set within a similar ornament on the arch. This is not in the strict sense a Sheela-na-gig but what is known as an 'acrobatic figure.' Carvings of a similar style are a common feature of Romanesque art in Britain and Europe, but this is the only example of this style of carving surviving in Ireland and is found in a particularly special context and location. The Nun's Chapel was erected by Derbforgaill N'Mhael Sechnaill, wife of Tigernán O'Ruairc, king of Bréifne, and according to an entry in the Annals of the Four Masters it was completed in 1167.

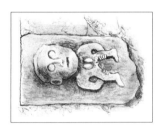

47. DOON – In Situ / On Castle

Doon Castle is on the east side of the Athlone to Birr road about a mile south of Ballynahown. This is a well-preserved figure carved in a reclining position on a quoin stone on the northeast corner of the tower to the left of the main entrance. The right hand passes underneath the thigh and the other over the left thigh. The legs are carved as standing but both feet point toward the right and there are two tiny breasts.

58. GARRY – In Situ / On Castle

Garry Castle is situated about midway along the Birr to Clonmacnoise road, between Cloghan and Banagher. This figure is about 35 ft / 12 m high on the east wall of the old castle and stands perched in a very precarious position as if ready to fall any day.

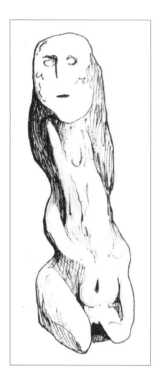

73. KNOCKARLEY—Private

This strange, dramatically sculpted figure is undoubtedly of the same genre as the Sheela-na-gigs, but is clearly a unique example. Its origins are unknown but was found near Knockharley which is only about 1.5 mi / 2.5 km southeast of the important old monastic center of Seir Kieran (100).

It is carved from a local sandstone and appears as if this particular piece was chosen for its shape, which the carver evidently modified using the existing contours. It is obviously a freestanding figure as it would have been nearly impossible to erect on a building, and its age is difficult to judge. Her face is inclined toward the right on top of an elongated neck, and although she is fairly weathered it is clear that her right hand lies across the belly and the left hand is laid on the thigh. The figure does not appear to have legs but there is a small yet clearly defined vulva marked by a small incision surrounded by a very thick raised oval. Like the Seir Kieran figure, there are small neat holes drilled into the top of her head and another below the vulva. Height: 55 cm.

75. LEMANAGH—Missing

The castle is three miles from Firbane on the road to Ballycumber. This figure was known from a drawing that existed in 1870 and belonged to Thomas Cooke of Birr, who wrote a history of the area and owned drawings of various other Sheela-na-gigs. Unfortunately both the drawing and the stone can no longer be found.

102. SEIR KIERAN — National Museum

The Sheela-na-gig from Seir Kieran is one of the most intriguing of the genre and is occasionally on display in the National Museum. It is very deeply sculpted and many of its features are well preserved. The most curious feature, however, is a series of eleven holes drilled through the figure's stomach, lower abdomen, and deep into the stone from the back of the head. In fact it is difficult to discern exactly which hole might represent a vulva.

The figure originates from an ancient and once very important monastic site that was founded by one of the greatest early saints of Ireland, Ciarán the Elder, a contemporary of Patrick. This once great monastic center was built within a large hilltop enclosure extending over twenty-five acres in which can be found the remains of a round tower, ancient tombstones and traces of earthworks. The site is the burial place of the ancient kings of Ossory, a kingdom that comprised Kilkenny and parts of Laois and Offaly, and which was a sacred center long before the Christian era.

Seir Kieran is in the village of Clareen about 4 mi / 6 km southeast of Birr on the R421 Kinnity to Roscrea road. The old church is now destroyed but the figure was depicted in the *Dublin Penny Journal* of 1834 as protruding from the eastern gable near 'an old freestone widow frame,' but was found later 'abutting on the vallum of the ancient enclosure.' This article also made reference to another figure in the west gable of the old church that was regarded as an image of St. Ciarán, but this has subsequently disappeared. 42 x 25 cm.

County Laois

7. BALLAGHMORE—In Situ / On Castle

Ballaghmore castle is situated about 4.5 mi / 7 km east of Roscrea and is operated as a commercial accommodation and activities center. The Sheela-na-gig can be seen on a quoin stone about 30 ft / 9 m from the ground, on the southwest tower wall of this late fifteenth-century castle. The left arm rests on the left thigh and the right arm appears to rest on the right hip. The feet are pointed and turned outwards, and the left foot appears also be slightly raised. According to John Feehan and George Cunningham, who recorded the figure in 1978, it is 'considerably weathered and sand grains at the surface are easily rubbed off,' and it does look quite worn.

46. CULLAHILL—In Situ / On Castle

Cullahill is on the old main Dublin to Cork road, now the R639, about 4 mi / 6 km southwest of Durrow. A heavily built and stern-looking Sheela-na-gig with broad shoulders but no legs is situated high up on the south wall of the peel tower. The breasts are fairly large and below them is deeply etched ribbing. Cullahill was one of the more important strongholds of the Fitzgeralds and the date given for its construction is 1425.

87. PORTNAHINCH—Missing

The castle from which this figure originates from has been totally destroyed and the Sheela-na-gig has been missing since the 1930s. The figure in a grainy photograph published in the anthropological periodical *Man* shows a figure that is 'standing, with legs awkwardly apart and arms slightly akimbo suggesting usual gesture toward the abdomen and a large, low-set head.' It was discovered at the same time as the Tinnakill figure (114) which has also gone missing.

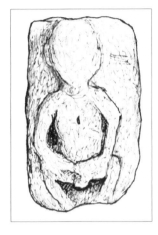

97. ROSENALLIS—National Museum

Rosenallis is about 4 mi / 6 km northwest of Mountmellick. The figure was discovered in 1992 in the Church of Ireland graveyard and removed to the National Museum. The stump of a round tower and other remnants, including the ruined church from which it is presumed the Sheela-na-gig originated, attest to the former importance of the site as an ancient holy center. The figure is carved from sandstone and is rather weathered with the facial features and other finer details obliterated, although there are still traces of ribbing below the small oval breasts. 51 x 31 cm.

104. SHANE CASTLE—Missing

John O'Donovan noted a figure that fits the description of a Sheela-na-gig on this castle in the mid-1800s but it has since gone missing. The castle is about 4 mi / 6 km east of Portlaoise.

113. TIMAHOE—Missing

Timahoe Castle is about 8 mi / 13 km southeast of Portlaoise and 5 mi / 8.5 km southwest of Stradbally. It is possible that there were formerly two figures on the castle, one of which was said to be 'a strange figure ... at the doorway.' According to information given to Dr. Edith Guest in the 1930s there was another on the north wall. The original information did not give a description of the figure, or figures, nor are there any illustrations. The castle has disintegrated a good deal and the north wall has since collapsed but it is possible that the figure or figures may still exist within the fallen rubble.

114. TINAKILL — Missing

This Sheela-na-gig, from the ruined castle at Timahoe, was discovered by Ms. Helen M. Roe, the early pioneer of Sheela-na-gig exploration, who identified the stone in a garden wall of a house near the river Dangan in Mountmellick. It is not certain what happened to the carving, but the photograph taken by Ms. Roe shows details of a standing figure with a long neck, straight, thin legs, the left hand indicating the genitals and the right hand raised to the head.

County Carlow

99. RUTLAND — Privately Owned

This Sheela-na-gig was originally thought to have come from Benkerry Castle but the researcher Gabriel Cannon discovered that it was found in a river somewhere in County Offaly in the 1940s. It is a very large and well-preserved figure carved onto a stone that is about 1 m x 0.5 m. The left hand points upwards and appears to be holding a pointed object while there is clear ribbing that extends across the chest area.

County Kildare

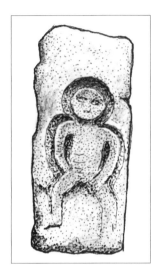

21. BLACK HALL—Privately Owned

Blackhall Castle is about 10 km south of Kilcullen and about 1.5 mi / 2 km north of Narraghmore. The Sheela-na-gig was set in stonework of recent origin by the doorway of the peel tower of the thirteenth-century castle facing southwest, but has been removed and is now kept by the owner of the castle. It is carved in low relief with a groove around the head, and her right leg is slightly raised. It appears as if both hands pass under the thighs and are joined in a gesture below the abdomen. The vulva is well defined and below this is a round indentation or shallow hole.

27. CARRICK—Missing

Around the turn of the century a figure called the 'Evil Eye Stone of the Castle' is known to have existed in the area. It was transferred along with the Murray Collection around that time to Cambridge University Museum of Archaeology and Ethnology in England, and has since disappeared.

63. KILDARE—In Situ / In Church

A small, nude cherub spreading her legs adorns the crypt in which was buried Bishop Arthur Wellesley, who obviously believed in the power of the feminine spirit. One must bend down to view her as she is set below the left corner of the top slab, above a crucifixion panel. This late sheela-like figure was identified by Mr. John Hunt and is carved in a much more naturalistic manner than the true Sheela-na-gigs. The funerary monument is thought to have been carved in

1539 and is now in St. Brigit's Cathedral which was built on the site of the monastery founded by St. Brigit in the fifth or sixth century. Why the Bishop had naked women on his crypt is not known.

County Westmeath

6. ATHLONE—Athlone Castle Museum

This is one of two Sheela-na-gigs currently retained in the Castle Museum in Athlone; the second is from Rahan (88). It was previously set up over a gateway to the laundry of the convent of St. Peter's Port, established in the eighteenth century, but is thought to have originated from the nearby twelfth-century Cluniac monastery of which not a trace now remains. The figure is carved in deep relief and is depicted with her arms embracing her tightly flexed legs, and she has a very distinct striated pattern incised across the left cheek.

26. CARNE CASTLE—National Museum

Found in the ruins of Carne Castle, at Coolatore, 1 mi / 1.5 km west of Moate, this Sheela-na-gig was acquired by the National Museum in 1956. Carne Castle was a sixteenth-century tower house, clan seat of the O'Melaghlin family whose ancestors were kings of Meath. It is a bulky figure with heavy shoulders and bulbous breasts, but an unusual feature is the widely splayed thighs with feet meeting at the heels. 63 x 36 cm.

32. CHLORAN—British Museum (Witt Collection)

This figure from the old church at Chloran was found in a field in 1859 on an estate known as Old Town. It was originally in the possession of Sir Benjamin Chapman of Killua Castle, Westmeath, and was subsequently acquired by the British Museum in 1865. In 1866 Thomas Wright recorded it in his book *The Worship of the Generative Powers During the Middle Ages of Western Europe*. It is thought to be made of a coarse-grained rock, possibly even granite, which would be unique and appears very akin to the Cavan Sheela-na-gig with similar depiction of ribs, teeth showing, the squatting position of its legs and the hands joined in a gesture around the extremely large genitalia, and there is a hole at the top of its head. 47 x 20 cm.

83. MOATE—In Situ / On Wall

Moate Castle is on the north side of the road going out of the village toward Kilbeggan. This strange little figure, only 3.35 cm high, is currently set in an oval sunk in cement over the gateway in the wall of the castle yard which was built in 1649. It has a wide mouth with thick lips showing teeth and a protruding tongue, a striated hairstyle, and a waist belt or band across the abdomen. Its style suggests that it might be of early Romanesque origin but its context suggests a later date.

88. RAHAN—Castle Museum, Athlone

According to D. Newman in his report to the Royal Society in 1972, this Sheela-na-gig was discovered 'sitting upright on the ruined walls of the chapel or church in the cemetery to the south of

St. Carthach's Church,' during grave-digging. Newman noted that it has been carved with 'vigour and attention to detail,' as much of the pockmarks can be seen. It is also a rare example of the type carved in the round with legs flexed up over the abdomen and revealing a very clearly defined vulva with an indented rim which appears as if it has been rubbed. The figure is also noted for its strong brow lines and its pronounced breasts under the arms. A second figure (No. 6) is also on display in the museum. 28 x 21 cm.

109. TAGHMON—In Situ / On Church

This very odd four-eyed Sheela-na-gig is situated above a trefoil window in the north wall of the fifteenth-century fortified manorial church of St. Munna. An arched stone roof and a four-story castellated tower have been added on to the western end which, together with the battlements on the older section, make the building look more like a castle than a church. There is a slight but distinct indication of the vulva on this curious crouched figure, with hands holding the legs. There is something like a beard beneath her mouth or perhaps it is a tongue, and apart from the holes in her head, which look like an extra pair of eyes, there is also a hole at the position of the bellybutton. It has been suggested that the extra pair of holes may have held horns. The Church is on the Mullingar–Castlepollard road about 1 mi / 1.5 km east of Crookedwood.

County Longford

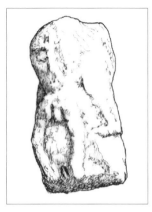

1. ABBEYLARA—In Situ / In Abbey
Abbeylara is a small village about 2 mi / 3 km east of Granard, and the ruins of the thirteenth-century Cistercian Abbey can be found on the east side of the village. A deeply sculpted but very weathered figure is protruding from the inside wall of a fifteenth-century tower. There are three deep indentations around the area of the breasts, and the pudenda are depicted by an oval depression with a raised middle strand. 36 x 21 cm.

92. RATHCLINE—In Situ, On Church
Rathcline Church is approx 2 mi / 3 km south of Lanesborough. The figure is carved on the cornerstone of one of the windows. The only indication that it could be considered as a Sheela-na-gig is the hole representing a vulva but it is otherwise difficult to classify. It is probably Romanesque in origin.

County Meath

5. ARDCATH—Private
Currently on a driveway wall at the entrance to a farm 1 mi / 1.5 km southwest of Ardcath. It is now rather badly weathered. The arms hang symmetrically across the body, and the hands, which have a faint suggestion of fingers, rest on the thighs close by the pudenda. In 1984, the figure was in private possession. 54 x 28 cm.

48. DOWTH — In Situ / On Church

The Sheela-na-gig is on the south wall of Dowth Old Church about 5 mi / 8 km southeast of Slane. You have to look hard to find it as it is now partly hidden behind the John Boyle O'Reilly memorial. The figure is very worn and has been badly damaged. When Dr. Guest visited the church in the 1930s she was disappointed to find that 'the prominent abdomen characteristic of this figure had been hacked off to accommodate a modern tombstone.' An earlier photograph confirms that the figure at one time had legs with her thighs splayed, with the hands directed toward her genitals. It was formerly known as an image of St. Seanachan.

62. KELLS — Missing

A female figure was recorded by Wilde (1857) in the catalogue of the Royal Irish Academy Collection as being in the church at Kells. Wilde was familiar with Sheela-na-gigs so this is most probably a valid record. Unfortunately, however, there is now no trace of the figure.

98. ROSNAREE — In Situ / In Old Mill

This Sheela-na-gig can be found only about 0.5 mi / 1 km west of the famous Brú na Bóinne Centre. The mill is on the site of a Cistercian monastery, and the figure was remembered by the former owner of the mill as an original goddess when visited by Margaret Murray in the early years of the twentieth century.

107. SUMMERHILL — Missing

A figure that appears from the description to be a Sheela-na-gig was recorded as being in a rock garden at Summerhill House, the seat of the Earl of Longford. This house is now a ruin and no figure is to be found.

110. TARA — In Situ / On Standing Stone

Possibly one of the most significant Sheela-na-gigs in Ireland can be seen on the east face of a standing stone in the churchyard at the ancient sacred site of Tara.

The figure is carved onto the tallest of a pair of standing stones, the other one being a squat, rounded pillar. These are regarded traditionally as the Blocc and Bluigne of mythology, between which the intended king of Ireland would pass on his way to the coronation site.

The figure is worn but carved in relief with the left leg straight down and the other bent inwards. It is hard to make out the position of the arms but she appears to be gesturing toward the genital area. There has been a good deal of speculation about the Tara figure; some have likened it to the figure of the god Cernunnos whereas others have disputed whether the figure is actually a Sheela-na-gig. The age of the figure and stone are perhaps the most contentious issues with dates varying from pre-Christian times to the later medieval period. Tara is the one of the most important sacred ceremonial centers of Ireland, so the existence of a Sheela-na-gig has deep implications.

The stone that the figure is carved onto is also known as St. Adamnan's Pillar, a name that commemorates the saint who is supposed to have championed the rights of women in a set of Brehon laws known as Adomnán's Law.

He also wrote the hagiography of St. Columba, the saint who established the monastic center at Iona and brought the Gaelic/Celtic church into Scotland in the sixth century.

County Dublin

50. DRIMNAGH—In Situ

This is a modern figure carved by unknown local masons restoring the church near Drimnagh castle. It is included here as many people who are not aware of its provenance assume it to be a 'real' Sheela-na-gig. However, it may be that the unknown mason may well be making up for the loss of other figures were noted in the area: one possible figure at Ballyfermot to the northwest, and another at Grangegorman, said to be on a gateway on Lwr Grangegorman Avenue. So many of the former buildings having been destroyed in the area, anything is possible.

78. LUSK—Missing

The antiquarian Austin Cooper recorded a figure fitting the description of a Sheela-na-gig at the church at Lusk in 1783. It is said that in 1844 the Rev. Mr. Tyrell buried presumably the figure then known as 'The Idol.' Cooper's description gives us an idea of the physical characteristics of the figure: 'the human features [were represented as] fancifully hideous; the face being 7 inches broad, and the head without neck or body, being attached to a pair of kneeling thighs and legs. It is likely that kneeling implies the kind of reduced body which is typical of the sheelas.'

81. MALAHIDE — In Situ / On Church

In 1954, P.J. Hartnett reported workers clearing up the church next to the castle (also known as 'The Abbey') for Lord Talbot de Malahide revealed a Sheela-na-gig on a quoin or cornerstone at the northeast angle of the old church. This is a fifteenth-century church dedicated to St. Sylvester, and the Sheela-na-gig is situated immediately below the roof at 'the springing of the gable.'

However, the figure is rapidly becoming only a vague outline of its former self. Features discernible on an early photograph are now not very clear at all, and there is a general deterioration of the whole figure that is frightening to contemplate. The fingers of the left hand rest on the thigh, but the other hand is not discernible, although there is a clear trace of the slit of the pudenda. In the same position on the opposite side of the church is another figure but this is too worn to ascertain exactly what it represents. 48 x 25 cm.

106. STEPASIDE — In Situ / On Standing Stone

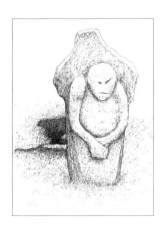

Situated on the public golf course, which is on the east side of the road going south just outside of Stepaside, in the middle of an old laneway lined with trees about 100 yds / 100 m to the east of the ruins of Jamestown House. It is the site of an early monastic settlement.

This strange figure looms out of a very old cross-shaped stone about 4 ft / 1.2 m tall by a little old well and is of a style that has been suggested

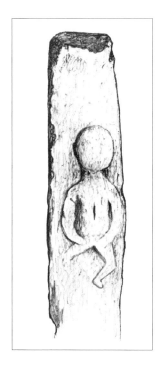

may be eighth-century or earlier. The figure has been carved in deep relief on the cross, head hanging low between powerful shoulders, and her vulva represented, or covered, by a very worn box-like object, though this is possibly her hands. On the reverse side of the stone are a circle and other symbolism now too worn to easily decipher by the naked eye but has been shown as a second figure in a Lidar scan (see Chapter 7).

108. SWORDS—National Museum

This Sheela-na-gig is carved on a tall limestone pillar stone of uncertain age that acted as a gatepost at Drynam House near Swords, County Dublin. The stone was removed to the National Museum as 'it was in danger of destruction by farm carts passing by,' and possibly flanked the doorway of one of the ruined buildings in the general vicinity. It is carved in high relief and one leg is raised as if the figure is doing a jig. The right hand gestures toward the vulva and the left behind the thigh. 67 x 28 cm.

County Louth

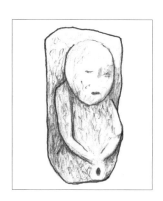

49. DROGHEDA—Millmount Museum

This rather worn Sheela-na-gig was originally on the wall of a house at No. 18 John Street in Drogheda and removed to the Millmount Museum when that part of town was demolished for road improvements. Ithell Colquhoun mentions being shown the figure in her 1954 book *The Crying of the Wind* so it appears that it was well-known at that time. It is thought to have come from the old town wall that once ran through this area. The hands are joined together just above a round hole or a depression which marks the genital area.

CONNAUGHT
County Sligo

19. BEHY—In Situ / On Farm Building/Private

The remains of Behy Castle are on the north side of the Sligo–Dublin road about 5 mi / 8 km south of Collooney and about 4 mi / 6 km north of Castlebaldwin. Only one wall of the castle is still standing but the Sheela-na-gig has been retained and at some stage was built into the gable of one of the outhouses of the farm. Later an additional shed was built extending the outhouse, which has acted as a roof covering the Sheela-na-gig, which results in this being perhaps the most well-preserved example in Ireland. All the finer details both of the carving itself and of the highly decorative nature of the dressing marks on the stone are clearly preserved. But the oddest feature is that the figure has, at some unknown date, been painted red, and has been this way for as long as anyone can remember, according to the owners of the farm. This paint looks very old and raises the possibility that painting Sheela-na-gigs may have been a more widespread practice. Oh for an analysis of that red paint.

85. MOYGARA — Missing

The castle is known as O'Gara's Fortress and is about 0.5 mi / 1 km from Lough Gara at its northwestern end. It is an impressive castle built during times of protracted troubles in the Connaght area, and after being attacked several times was finally burned down by Scottish mercenaries in 1581. The Sheela-na-gig is said to have been on the barbican over the entrance and to have been part of a pair of 'inverted pyramid shape' corbel stones.

Guest records that 'the limestone block, on the corbelled end of which the figure is rudely carved, now lies on the ground near the castle entrance,' and published a picture of the stone lying in the grass. Unfortunately, Guest's photograph is rather unclear, and there is now a heap of rubble piled up beneath the entrance and the stone has so far not been located. Weir described an acrobatic or dancing figure on one stone and on the corresponding corbel stone, a 'couple apparently coupling.' Anderson similarly records a figure with one arm held to the side of the head and the opposite leg raised high.

County Roscommon

35. CLOGHAN — In Situ / On Castle

Both this site and site 111 Taghboy are close to the same small road that goes from Ballyforan to Four Roads, which is a crossroads on a sharp bend of the R357 about 3 mi / 4.5 km south of Athleague (turn left from the N63 about 0.5 mi / 1 km south of Athleague). The route from the south is easier. Take the road going north in Ballyforan village. Site 108 is about 1.5 mi / 2.5 km north of Ballyforan, and Cloghan is about 1 mi / 1.5 km north of this.

Much of the old castle has been dismantled, but the tower with its well-preserved Sheela-na-gig is intact. It is carved on a quoin stone some distance from the ground on the southeast corner of the tower and is in a reclining position. She gestures both hands toward a clearly defined vulva, and there appears to be a secondary vulva-like shape carved into the background just below this. Perhaps the most curious features are that she is the only Sheela-na-gig in Ireland with a protruding tongue, and the head is framed in some kind of headpiece. 60 x 30 cm.

52. EMLAGH MOR — In Situ / On Church

This figure is kept at Tempe House which is about 4 mi / 8 km northwest of Roscommon on the south side of the N60. It appears to have been originally a corbel of a possibly Romanesque church that formerly stood in the vicinity. It is very worn but can be seen to have the main characteristics of a Sheela-na-gig, but with legs twisted back in an acrobat-like posture.

89. RAHARA — Roscommon Museum

The old church of Rahara from where this figure originates is about 8 mi / 13 km southeast of Roscommon town on the Athlone to Athleague road, but it is kept in the County Museum, in Roscommon town.

The Sheela-na-gig came to light during cleaning-up work being carried out in the graveyard when a voussoir-shaped stone with one face deeply sunken into the ground was found. On turning it over it was discovered that it had a female figure carved on it, and because of the stone being face downwards in the soil, the fine details had been kept in excellent condition. It is carved in low relief, has quite large breasts and very pronounced nostril channels. Both arms are clearly shown reaching down beneath the widely splayed thighs. This figure has many similarities to the Ballinderry figure (9) being also surrounded by a Celtic design which falls down to her arms like a hair decoration. It was also carved into a wedge-shaped stone which denotes that it would have been a keystone and was probably erected over a doorway. 45 x 40 cm.

100–101. SCREGG—In Situ / On Coach House

Scregg is about 6.5 mi / 10 km southeast of Roscommon and about 1.5 mi / 2 km south of Knockcroghery. The two figures at Scregg probably both originated from the old castle, a tower house of the Ui Maine clan, most of which has now been dismantled. The present structure on the site of the castle is a very grand period house, and the Sheela-na-gigs have been re-erected on either side of the entrance to a carriage house which is built of stone from the old castle. One of the figures is very small, being only about 10 cm high, and is depicted with legs widely splayed in an almost acrobatic fashion. The larger figure is just under 35 cm high and would have formed a keystone, possibly over a window or door. This figure is depicted in a posture similar to the Ballinderry sheela but has ears that are strikingly similar to the cow ears of the figure at Kilsarkan (68) in Kerry. Scregg is less than 2.5 mi / 4 km to the northeast of Rahara church and it is curious that four out of the five Sheela-na-gigs in Roscommon are found grouped within a small area of less than 4 mi / 6 km radius of each other. The fifth, Emlagh Mor (52), which is outside of this immediate area, is also of a distinctly different class.

111. TAGHBOY — In Situ / On Church

One of the most curious Sheela-na-gigs in the country was revealed when ivy was removed from the western gable of Taghboy church. The figure is carved on a pyramidal-shaped stone on the apex of the gable and is the only Sheela-na-gig so far discovered that is situated in such a position. Perhaps the reason why she is sitting so high up is that she also has another very curious feature below her vulva, which does very much resemble male genital organs. See Site 35 Cloghan for directions to this site.

County Galway

9. BALLINDERRY — In Situ / On Castle

Ballinderry castle is about 4 mi / 6 km south of Tuam on the west side of the R347, the old Tuam–Athenry road. It can be seen from the road but may be obscured by forestry. The Sheela-na-gig is on the keystone of the archway of the main doorway of this mid-sixteenth-century castle, said to be the last built of the Galway/Clare castles. It is a distinctive and very important example as the figure is depicted on a background of Celtic-style patterns, which is a unique feature. Only two other Sheela-na-gigs with any kind of Celtic decoration have been so far identified. One is the figure from Rahara church (89) and a second was only discovered in the spring of 2018 in the east of the county, Clootymurraghy (42).

The Ballinderry figure is surrounded by decoration that includes Celtic knotwork based on three strands passing behind the head of the figure, and a triskele or triquetra, a sexafoil rose and a marigold motif divided into eight divisions. Recent Lidar scans have shown the figure of a bird, a duck or swan, in the top right of the figure. The breasts are like folds under the armpits and the hands are joined in a gesture around the vulva, out of which appears to be a rush of liquid, perhaps indicating her connection to the mythic river hag. 25 x 35 cm.

42. CLOOTYMURRAGHY — Private

This figure only very recently came to light having been set up on a farmyard building for an unknown length of time. It is also unknown how it arrived there or where it came from, and was only revealed in 2018 to a local researcher. It is however a very important figure, being one of only three Sheela-na-gigs depicted with associated Celtic knotwork, the others being from the castle at Ballinderry (9), and Rahara (89). The location of this figure is actually about midway between the castle at Ballinderry and the church at Rahara, and one cannot but speculate whether there is a direct connection, the same artist/carver perhaps. It is also one of only three with a protruding tongue and there is also something that looks like a nose ring.

82. MERLIN PARK—In Situ / On Castle

At about 60 cm this is one of the smallest Sheela-na-gigs and is impossible to see without a telescopic lens of some kind. This figure is a part of the detail within the overall patterning on the carved lintel of a window on the south wall of the castle. Doughiska Castle is on the west side of Mater Park Hospital on the Old Dublin / Oranmore road east of Galway city.

County Mayo

3. AGHAGOWER—In Situ / On Holy Well

This small figure was found during work on the nearby graveyard and is now erected on the wall enclosure of St. Patrick's well on the west side of the village.

45. CROSS—In Situ / In Church

This rather worn figure is one of the more recent to come to light, and is kept in the church at Cross on R334 Headford–Ballinrobe road. It was apparently brought to the church in 1987 after being found on a coach house in the area. Its origins before that are unknown. A second figure in the village of Hollymount, not more than 10 km to the north of the Cross figure, has been revealed in the final days of the production of this book.

61. HOLLYMOUNT—In Situ

This figure was revealed in an article in *Archaeology Ireland* Issue 121, Autumn 2017, just as this book was nearing completion. It is typical of the study of our Sheela-na-gigs that they keep turning up, making the compilation of lists almost impossible but showing that the time has come for them to reveal themselves.

Hollymount village is about 8 km northeast of Ballinrobe on the R331 Claremorris road. Erected on a small park feature by an old water pump by the entrance to the GAA field, she is one of only about half a dozen figures that is wearing a hat. Even more unusual is the way her legs are widely splayed and feet upturned, with what may be pointed shoes. She shares this posture with only two other figures (Scregg and Kilsarkan). The figure was removed to its present location from a wall on land where a former castle stood about 1.6 km away. Its origin is unknown.

105. SHOODAUN, Church, In Situ

Badly worn figure kept in the local church. Recently recognised as a Sheela-na-gig by a reliable researcher but no image yet available.

ULSTER
County Cavan

31. CAVAN—Cavan County Museum

This Sheela-na-gig can be seen along with the Lavey figure (72) and other interesting items

in the Cavan County Museum in Ballyjamesduff. Unfortunately, there is no record of the church from which it is said to have originated and it is probably no longer in existence. The knees are widely splayed and hands are joined in a gesture around the extremely large genitalia below which is a hole. The right side is badly damaged but she retains many interesting features, particularly the beading or bands around the forehead and around the lips, as well as a slightly protruding tongue, features possibly lost by weathering on other examples. 43 x 23 cm.

74. LAVEY — Cavan County Museum

This figure, carved on a limestone slab, was found in 1842 by a Dr. Charles Halpin, laid loosely on a gate pier at the entrance to the old graveyard at Lavey church, and was thought by the finder to have been a quoin stone. Lavey church is thought to date no earlier than the late twelfth century and is dedicated to St. Dymphna, an early Irish saint who is patroness of the insane. One of the most interesting aspects of this figure is the unidentified discoid object, which appears to be located under her left arm, yet confusingly the outline of the circle is also incised twice on top of her arm. The fingers of the large hands rest on the raised rim of a box-like slit of the pudenda and she has deeply set eyes, indications of teeth and extremely long toes on turned-out feet. 47 x 58 cm.

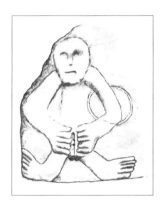

115. TOOMREGAN — In Situ / On Church

This is a most peculiar and rather ambiguous figure, with a large scowling face and sagging

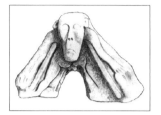

genitalia. There are differing opinions whether this figure is carved in the Sheela-na-gig tradition or not. Her or his right hand is shown as normal with fingers marked, and her left hand appears to be holding some unidentifiable object.

It may have been part of the outer face of a narrow, splayed, round-headed window. It was found in a ditch in 1961 near the site of the early monastery of Toomregan (Tuaim Drecon), founded by St. Bricin in the seventh century, where traces of both a church and a round tower survive.

Tuaim Drecon was as an old druidical or bardic school and early Christian monastery. This was a well-renowned school of learning where law, history and especially medicine were taught. St. Bricin was famous for 'the trepanning of skulls.'

Now sitting inside the doorway to Toomregan Church of Ireland Church, Ballyconnell, which is about 6 km west of Belturbet. 60 x 70 cm.

County Donegal

44. CORVEEN — Missing

Corveen or Lough Eske Castle, the island stronghold of the O'Donnells, is a few miles east of Donegal town, but the Sheela-na-gig is now unfortunately missing despite several very thorough searches made in recent years. Thomas Fagan's 'Ordnance Survey Letters of 1846–7' records a 'female exhibitionist figure' which was said to have been originally on the older castle in the lake and had been re-erected on the coach house of the new castle on the mainland.

Fortunately, he made a fairly good sketch of the figure. It appears to have been an important emblem of the O'Donnells, for them to have re-erected it on their new base on the mainland.

County Fermanagh

79. LUSTYMORE—In Situ / In Churchyard

On Boa Island, at the northern end of Lower Lough Erne, is the ancient church site of Caldragh, which has been the depository of a number of ancient artifacts over the recent century. Most notable of these is the double-headed figure known as the Janus Figure. Placed close to this is the less well-known Sheela-na-gig from nearby Lustymore Island, site of an early monastery.

The figure is somewhat similar in style to the Janus Figure; features such as the pointed chin and the broad open mouth give the appearance that the figure is carved in the same tradition.

The left eye is either damaged or imperfect, perhaps deliberately represented as closed or blind, and the legs of this figure are also too worn to make out. The vulva is no longer clearly marked but the hands are depicted in the classic posture directed toward the lower abdomen.

Lough Erne is famous for a number of carved figures that have been found in association with early churches on the islands in the lake. See Addendum.

County Derry

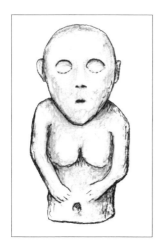

80. MAGHERA—In Situ / On Church

About 6 m from the ground on the northern side of the tower of the old church at Maghera is a Sheela-na-gig set among the masonry. Unfortunately, the lower part of the sculpture appears to have broken away, although the gesture of the hands toward the lower abdomen is clear.

County Down

4. AGHALURCHER—Enniskillen Museum

Aghalurcher Church is about 3 km south of Lisnaskea and west of the main Newtownbutler road. A Romanesque-type figure was discovered here in 1970, with a large head and legs raised in the acrobatic fashion, heels touching ears, presumably female. A report on the figure surmised that the stone was cut in such a way that it formed the under-section of a cornice or a gable-coping rather than a corbel. There are remains of a medieval church on the site of a foundation established by St. Ronan in the seventh century, and on the gateway leading into the churchyard is a good example of a Romanesque head.

72. KIRKISTOWN—Missing

Three figures were reported as coming from this late castle built by the Savages, none of which can now be located. It appears from the record that at least one of them was more than possibly a Sheela-na-gig.

County Tyrone

53. ERRIGAL KEEROGE I—Ulster Museum

Two figures have come from the early church of St. Dachiarog, situated in the Clogher Valley about 5.5 km west of Ballygawley. One is now located in the Ulster Museum, Belfast, and the second (53) was discovered during research by the present author and is still on site.

The church is situated on a hilltop thought to be the ancient site of a Celtic shrine or sanctuary. It is mainly associated with St. Ciarán and it is comparable in importance to his main center of Seir Kieran in Tipperary.

When this figure was first handed in to the museum it was described as having come from somewhere else other than the church, but an investigation later discovered its actual place of origin.

Andersen commented on the 'impressive ugliness' of this carving, and it is certainly not intended as a portrait of beauty with her large, bald head, crooked nose and wide mouth. The hands are directed in a gesture toward the pudenda with the right hand passing beneath one thigh and the other hand passing from in front. Deliberate asymmetry is also at play here with one shoulder raised higher than the other and one breast is longer than the other. 46 x 25 cm.

54. ERRIGAL KEEROGE II—In Situ / In Churchyard

The second figure from this important site came to light during research in the late 1990s and had previously been unreported. The Sheela-na-gig has been built into the low masonry that

constitutes the remains of the old church and is over 60 cm high and carved from a dark grey sandstone. The figure is carved in quite high relief and is depicted squatting with arms reaching straight down to the abdomen, with deeply carved indentations beneath legs and arms. The head is represented by a recessed circular depression above the body and there is a deep groove on the stone to the left of her, giving the impression of having been carved for a particular function. Another crack running from this carved notch to the left cheek gives the impression of a pipe-smoking Sheela-na-gig. Unfortunately she is rather worn or weathered in the lower areas so that the hands and details of the area around the pudenda are unclear.

ADDENDUM

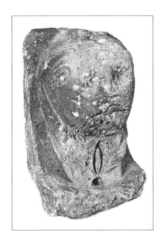

A SHEELA-NA-GIG SOLD AT AUCTION

The origins of this Sheela-na-gig are unknown and its current whereabouts are a mystery, so we do not even know if it originated from Ireland, and the buyer has left us no record of its current whereabouts. The figure came to public attention when it turned up for auction in Dublin and was subsequently sold in May 2003. It is now known only from photographs supplied by Adam's auctioneers.

This is a unique Sheela-na-gig; it appears to be legless and in fact consists predominantly of a large head, arms faintly visible, a well-defined vulva, and a hole that one can only presume represents the anus. The figure may have been carved as a corbel.

Figures That May Be of the Sheela-Na-Gig Tradition

The following are a selection of figures that were originally classed as Sheela-na-Gigs but which are no longer regarded as falling within this category, although many may still be related to a similar tradition.

ARMAGH

A female figure, once listed as a Sheela-na-gig, was found in the Chapter house of Armagh Cathedral that was said to have been 'dug up many years ago when digging a grave in the Cathedral yard.' Andersen did not consider the figure as a Sheela-na-gig, for she is depicted with a skirt, round breasts, a bow lifted behind her head and a close-fitting cap.

BALLYCLOGHDUFF, County Westmeath

Located 4.5 km east-northeast of Carne Castle, on the gatepost of a former mill can be found what has become known as a Sean-na-Gig. The right arm is holding an over-large downward-pointing object that is presumed to be a penis, and the left arm reaches across his chest holding an object of some kind. A diamond or chevron is distinctly carved on the middle of the chest and, unusually, the figure has inward-pointing feet.

CARNDONAGH, County Donegal

The eighth–ninth century Carndonagh cross with its two 'guardian stones' are now kept in a safe place, a roofed platform beside the Church which will hopefully protect them against the ravages of the weather, and being freestanding allows full view of all sides of the carved stones.

A figure carved in low relief on one of these stones is very difficult to interpret due to the wear of countless years, but its main features are a large head, large hands held open over the abdomen, and an indentation where the genitals would be, which suggested to H.C. Lawler, when he visited the site in the 1930s, that it was a Sheela-na-gig. Although a very interesting carving, it is difficult to ascertain if it is closely related to the Sheela-na-gigs.

CASHEL, County Tipperary

Originally found in the cathedral at Cashel is a very curious stone which Guest included in her 1936 list but which cannot be truly said to be a Sheela-na-gig, but for which 'Cat Goddess' would be a better name. There is no reference to the genitals, but the facial features are reminiscent of the early tradition of tattooing. She is carved as a caryatid, intended for some supporting function on a building, and is armless with twisted legs, a fat belly and poignant breasts.

CASTLEMAGNER, County Tipperary

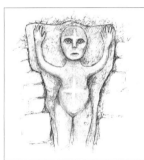

Castlemagner is about 8 km southeast of Kanturk near Ceciltown. On the north side of the road about 1 km west of Castlemagner is a path by the river Caltra which leads to the well. Flanking the opening of a popular Holy Well dedicated to St. Brigit is what is thought to be a later Sheela-na-gig, whilst on the opposite side is another much smaller figure which has been likened to a Roman soldier.

The figure is standing or kneeling with her arms raised, and her face is unusually well rendered with large staring almond-shaped eyes and deeply incised mouth. Andersen suggested 'an adaptation of the sheela idea by a polite age,' and refers to Du Noyer's estimate of an age of around the seventeenth century. The tradition of rubbing the figure with a pebble or stone has left well-worn cross marks on the forehead, hands, belly and thighs.

CLONMACNOISE, County Offaly

On the south side of the tenth-century north cross at Clonmacnoise is a figure with entwining legs that has been described as Cernunnos-like. It was included in the 1894 list of Sheelas and later classed by Edith Guest as a 'Sheela-na-Gig of a type not hitherto found.' It is probably of a closely related tradition to the Cat figure in Cashel.

GREY ABBEY, County Down

A figure described as 'a male Sheela-na-gig which lacks a penis' can be found on a Romanesque corbel table in the Abbey.

KILCARNE, County Meath

A supposed Sheela-na-gig carved on the old font in the church of Kilcarne near Johnstown was recorded by Wakeman in 1879, but does not fall within this category. A photograph published by Andersen shows 'an erotic theme consisting of a remarkable encounter between two or three people.'

KINSALE, County Cork

A figure can be found on a detached tombstone which is standing against the interior wall of the church of St. Multose. Also on the slab are funerary inscriptions dating the stone to the 1700s. Although this may not be classed amongst the Sheela-na-gigs it is a curious and very unusual carving which almost certainly owes much to the same tradition.

SHANE'S CASTLE, County Antrim

The antiquarian H.C. Lawlor refers to several figures known to him, one of which was at Shane's Castle, County Antrim. This was known as 'the Luck stone of the O'Neills,' but Anderson could find only 'The Black Head of the O'Neills.' Lawlor also tantalisingly refers to three figures of a similar kind in Savage's Castle, Kirkistown, County Down.

WHITE ISLAND, County Fermanagh

On White Island there are a number of strange stone figures which probably originate from the early Christian sanctuaries which existed on several of the islands of Lough Erne. One of the figures was formerly listed as a Sheela-na-gig due to its hands being crossed over the abdomen. It is approximately two feet long and she wears a short cloak-like mantle, a rheno, or secular dress. The legs are crossed but due to a lack of explicit reference to the vulva, it cannot be said to fall into the category of Sheela-na-gigs. However, this tenth-century figure could well be an early prototype. One workman employed to clean up the church site took such a dislike to it that he knocked the corner off one side of the figure. Another strange figure has what looks like three feet and arms that all point to the center, a stance that could also be related to the pose of the Sheela-na-gigs.

LIST OF KNOWN
SHEELA-NA-GIGS

ABBEYLARA, Co. Longford ....Church / In Situ

AGHADOE CASTLE, Co. Cork ....Castle / On Dovecote

AGHAGOWER, Co. Mayo ....Church site /On Well

AGHALURCHER, Co. Fermanagh...Church / Storage

ARDCATH, Co. Meath...Origin Unknown / (Private)

ATHLONE, Co. Westmeath ....Church / Castle Museum Athlone

BALLAGHMORE, Co. Laoise ....Castle / In Situ

BALLINACARRIGA, Co. Cork ....Castle / In Situ

BALLINDERRY CASTLE, Co. Galway ....Castle / In Situ

BALLEEN LITTLE, Co. Kilkenny ....Castle / In Situ

BALLYFINBOY CASTLE, Co. Tipperary.................................Castle / In Situ

BALLYLARKIN CHURCH, Co. Kilkenny ....Church / National Museum

BALLINACLOGH, Co. Tipperary ....Castle / In Situ

BALLYNAHINCH, Co. Tipperary....................................Castle / In Situ

BALLYNAMONA, Co. Cork ....Castle / Missing

BALLYPORTRY CASTLE, Co. Clare................. Castle / Clare County Museum Ennis

BALLYVOURNEY, Co. Cork ....Church / In Situ

BARNAHEALY, Co. Cork ....Castle / Missing

BEHY, Co. Sligo ....Castle / Re-erected on Outhouse

BIRR, Co. Offaly...............................Original Location Unknown / National Museum

BLACKHALL, Co. Kildare ....Castle / In Situ

BUNRATTY, Co. Clare...Castle / Re-erected in Main Hall

BURGESBEG I, Co. Tipperary ....Church / National Museum

BURGESBEG II, Co. Tipperary....................................Church / In Storage

CAHERELLY EAST, Co. Limerick.................................Hunt Museum Limerick

CARNE CASTLE, Co. Westmeath..Castle / National Museum

CARRICK CASTLE, Co. Kildare ....Castle / Missing

CASHEL I, Co. Tipperary ....In Situ on Bishops Palace

CASHEL II ....Cashel Arms Hotel. Possibly from Castle / House

CASTLE WIDENHAM, Co. Cork .... Holy Well / Private

CAVAN, Co. Cavan ....Church / National Museum / Cavan Co. Museum

CHLORAN, Co. Westmeath .... British Museum

CLENAGH, Co. Clare ....Castle / In Situ

CLOGHAN CASTLE, Co. Offaly ....Castle / Missing

CLOGHAN, Co. Roscommon...Castle / In Situ

CLOMANTAGH, Co. Kilkenny..Castle / In Situ

CLONBULLOGE, Co. Offaly ....Original Location Unknown / Private
CLONLARA, Co. Clare... Castle / On Canal Bridge
CLONMACNOISE, Co. Offaly ....Church / In Situ
CLONMEL, Co. Tipperary..Church / National Museum
CLONOULTY, Co. Tipperary...Church / Bolton Library, Cashel
CLOOTYMURRAGHY, East Galway .... Privately Owned
COOLIAGH MORE, Co. Kilkenny .... Roth House, Kilkenny
CORVEEN, Co. Donegal...Castle / Missing
CROSS, Co. Mayo.. In Church, Origin Unknown
CULLAHILL, Co. Laois..Castle / In Situ
DOON, Co. Offaly ....Castle / In Situ
DOWTH, Co. Meath ....Church / In Situ
DROGHEDA, Co. Louth ....Town Wall / Millmount Museum Drogheda
DRIMNAGH, Dublin... In Situ / Modern / On Church
DUNNAMAN, Co. Limerick ....Castle / In Situ
EMLAGH MOR, Co. Roscommon .... In Situ / Origin Church
ERRIGAL KEEROGE I, Co. Tyrone.........................Church / Ulster Museum, Belfast
ERRIGAL KEEROGE II, Co. Tyrone ....Church / On Site
FANTASTOWN, Co. Limerick ....Castle / In Situ
FETHARD WALL, Co. Tipperary...Town Wall / In Situ
FETHARD ABBEY, Co. Tipperary...Church / In Situ
GARRY, Co. Offaly ....Castle/ In Situ
GLANWORTH CASTLE, Co. Cork...Castle / In Storage
HOLYCROSS ABBEY, Co. Tipperary ....Church / In Situ
HOLLYMOUNT, Co. Mayo .... In Village
KELLS, Co. Meath ....Church / Missing
KILDARE, Co. Kildare ....Church / In Situ
KILLALOE, Co. Clare .... Church / Private
KILLINABOY CHURCH, Co. Clare ....Church / In Situ
KILMACOMMA, Co. Waterford ....Original Location Unknown / Missing
KILMOKEA, Co. Wexford ....National Museum / Church?
KILSARKAN, Co. Kerry ....Church / In Situ
KILSHANE, Co. Tipperary .... Church
KILTINANE CHURCH, Co. Tipperary ....Church / Missing
KILTINANE CASTLE, Co. Tipperary........................ Castle / On Well House / Private
KIRKISTOWN, Co. Down...Missing
KNOCKARLEY, Co. Offaly ....Original Location Unknown / Private
LAVEY, Co. Cavan ....Church / National Museum
LEMANAGHAN CASTLE, Co. Offaly ....Castle / Missing
LIATHMOR, Co. Tipperary ....Church / In Situ
LIXNAW, Co. Kerry...Castle / Kerry County Museum?
LUSK, Co. Dublin..Church / Missing

LUSTYMORE, Co. Fermanagh ....Church / Caldragh Graveyard
MAGHERA, Co. Derry...Church / In Situ
MALAHIDE, Co. Dublin..Church / In Situ
MERLIN PARK, Co. Galway...In Situ / On Castle
MOATE, Co. Westmeath...Castle / In Situ
MOYCARKEY, Co. Tipperary...Castle / Missing
MOYGARA, Co. Sligo... Doubtful but reliably recorded?
NEWTOWN LENNAN, Co. Tipperary..................................Church / National Museum
PORTNAHINCH, Co. Laois ....Castle / Missing
RAHAN, Co. Offaly ....Church / Castle Museum, Athlone
RAHARA, Co. Roscommon......................... Church / Roscommon County Museum
RANDALSTOWN, Co. Antrim ....Shane's Castle / Missing
RATH (Rath Blathmac), Co. Clare ....Church / In Situ
RATHCLINE, Co. Longford ....Church / In Situ
RATOO, Co. Kerry...Round Tower / In Situ
REDWOOD CASTLE, Co. Tipperary..Castle / In Situ
RINGASKIDDY, Co. Cork...............................Location Unknown / Cork City Museum
ROCHESTOWN, Co. Tipperary...Church / Missing
ROSENALLIS, Co. Laois... Church / Nat. Museum, Dublin
ROSNAREE, Co. Meath ....Mill / In Situ
RUTLAND, Co. Carlow...Originally from a river in Offaly
SCREGG A, Co. Roscommon .... Castle
SCREGG B...Two figures here on coach house
SEIR KIERAN, Co. Offaly...Church / Nat. Museum Dublin
SHANRAHAN, Co. Tipperary ....Church / In Situ
SHANE'S CASTLE, Co. Antrim...Missing
SHOODAUN, Co. Galway .... (Athenry)
STEPASIDE, Co. Dublin...Holy Well / In Situ
SUMMERHILL, Co. Meath ....Original Location Unknown / Missing
SWORDS, Co. Dublin ....Original Location Unknown / Nat. Museum
TAGHMON, Co. Westmeath ....Church / In Situ
TARA, Co. Meath ....Pillar Stone / In Situ
TAUGHBOY, Co. Roscommon ....On Apex of Church
THURLES, Co. Tipperary..Town Wall / In Situ
TIMAHOE, Co. Laois ....Castle / Missing
TINAKILL, Co. Laois ....Castle / Missing
TOOMREGAN, Co. Cavan ....In Situ / Church
TRACTON ABBEY, Co. Cork ....Church / Cork City Museum
TULLAROAN, Co. Kilkenny.. Unknown
TULLOVIN, Co. Limerick ....Castle / In Situ

REFERENCES AND FURTHER READING

Andersen, J. *The Witch on the Wall*. London 1977

Aarsleff, K. *Troldsten in Guds Hus*. www.menmyst.dk 2011

Berresford Ellis, P. *Celtic Women*. London 1995

_____. *The Druids*. London 1994

Barrow, G.I. *The Round Towers of Ireland*. Academy Press, Dublin 1979

Bahn, P. *Cave Art*. London 2007

Callan, M.B. *The Templars, the Witch and the Wild Irish*. Dublin 2015

Cherry, S. "Sheela-na-gigs from County Cork." *JCAHS*

_____*A Guide to Sheela-na-gigs*. National Museum, Dublin 1992

Clark, R. "Irish Goddesses from the Morrighan to Cathleen ni Houlihan." *Irish Literary Studies*, No. 34, 1991

Cherici, P. *Celtic Sexuality*. London 1995

Conderen, M. *The Serpent and the Goddess*. London 1989

Cook, J. *Ice Age Art*. British Museum 2013

Dobson, D. "Primitive Figures on Churches." *Man*, Vol XXX, 1930

Gimbutas, M. *The Language of the Goddess*. New York 1989

_____ *The Living Goddess*. California Press 1999

Goode, S. *Sheela-na-gig, Dark Goddess of Sacred Power*. Inner Traditions, Vermont 2016

Green, M. *Symbol and Image in Celtic Religion*. London 1989

Guest, E. "Irish Sheela-na-gigs in 1935." *JRSAI*, Vol VI 1936

____"Some Notes on Dating of Sheela-na-gigs." *JRSAI*, Vol VII 1937

____"Ballyvourney and its Sheela-na-gig." *Folklore*, Vol XLVIII 1937

____"A Sheela-na-gig at Clonmacnoise." *JRSAI*, Vol 84 1954

Hickey, H. *Images of Stone*. Belfast 1976

Jackson, S. *Celtic and Other Stone Heads*. London 1973

Jerman, J. *The Sheela-na-gig Carvings of the British Isles*. County Louth Archaelogical Society 1981

Kelly, E.P. *Sheela-na-gigs, Origins and Function*. National Museum, Dublin 1996

Kohl, J.G. *Reisen in Irland*. Vol 2. Dresden 1843

Lawlor, H.C. "Grotesque Carvings Improperly Called Sheela-na-gigs." *Irish Naturalists Journal*, Vol I. 1927

Lubell, W.M. *The Metamorphosis of Baubo*. London 1994

MacCana, P. *Celtic Mythology*. London 1985

Minihane, J. *The Christian Druids*. Dublin

Murray, M. "Female Fertility Figures." *Journal of the Royal Anthropological Society,* Vol 64. London 1934

Ni Donmhnaill, N. *Sheela in Her Cabin.* Irish Museum of Modern Art. Dublin 1994

O'Catháin, S. *The Festival of Brigit.* DBA Publications, Dublin 1995

O'Connor, J. *Sheela-na-gig.* Fethard Historical Society. 1991

O'Donovan, J. Ordnance Survey Letters, Royal Irish Academy, Dublin.

Pollack, R. *The Body of the Goddess.* London 2003

Rynne, E. "A Pagan Celtic Background for Sheela-na-gigs?" *Essays in Honour of Helen M Roe.* Ireland 1987

Sjöö, M. *The Norse Goddess.* Penzance, Kernow 2000

Smyth, D. *A Guide to Irish Mythology.* Irish Academic Press. 1988

Stokes, G.T. "Figures known as Hags of the Castles." *JRSAI,* Vol XXIV. 1984

Weir, A. & J. Jerman. *Images of Lust.* London 1986

Windele, J. *Topography of Cork West & North east.* Royal Irish Academy.

For an update of newly discovered figures:

www.irelands-sheelanagigs.org

www.sheelanagig.org

Catalogues and information about figures in Britain:

www.beyond-the-pale.org.uk

INDEX TO THE SHEELA-NA-GIGS

The Figures are also listed alphabetically with details of current location on Pages 178–180